T0251478

Public Library Collection Development in the Information Age

Public Library Collection Development in the Information Age has been co-published simultaneously as *The Acquisitions Librarian*, Number 20 1998.

Public Library Collection Development in the Information Age

Annabel K. Stephens
Editor

Public Library Collection Development in the Information Age has been co-published simultaneously as *The Acquisitions Librarian*, Number 20 1998.

CRC Press
Taylor & Francis Group
Boca Raton London New York

CRC Press is an imprint of the
Taylor & Francis Group, an informa business

Public Library Collection Development in the Information Age has been co-published simultaneously as *The Acquisitions Librarian*™, Number 20 1998.

Reprinted 2009 by CRC Press

The development, preparation, and publication of this work has been undertaken with great care. However, the publisher, employees, editors, and agents of The Haworth Press and all imprints of The Haworth Press, Inc., including The Haworth Medical Press® and Pharmaceutical Products Press®, are not responsible for any errors contained herein or for consequences that may ensue from use of materials or information contained in this work. Opinions expressed by the author(s) are not necessarily those of The Haworth Press, Inc.

The Haworth Press, Inc., 10 Alice Street, Binghamton, NY 13904-1580 USA

Cover design by Thomas J. Mayshock Jr.

Library of Congress Cataloging-in-Publication Data

Public library collection development in the information age / Annabel K. Stephens, editor.
  p. cm.
"Has been co-published simultaneously as The acquisitions librarian, no. 20, 1998."
Includes bibliographical references and index.
ISBN 0-7890-0528-X (acid-free paper) ISBN 0-7890-1336-3 (pbk: acid-free paper)
  1. Public libraries–Collection development–United States. 2. Libraries–United States–Special collections–Electronic information resources. I. Stephens, Annabel K. II. Acquisitions librarian.

Z687.2.U6P83 1998   98-7845
025.2'1–dc21   CIP

INDEXING & ABSTRACTING

Contributions to this publication are selectively indexed or abstracted in print, electronic, online, or CD-ROM version(s) of the reference tools and information services listed below. This list is current as of the copyright date of this publication. See the end of this section for additional notes.

- *Central Library & Documentation Bureau,* International Labour Office, CH-1211 Geneva 22, Switzerland

- *CNPIEC Reference Guide: Chinese National Directory of Foreign Periodicals,* P.O. Box 88, Beijing, People's Republic of China

- *Combined Health Information Database (CHID),* National Institutes of Health, 3 Information Way, Bethesda, MD 20892-3580

- *Current Awareness Abstracts,* Association for Information Management, Information House, 20-24 Old Street, London, EC1V 9AP, England

- *Educational Administration Abstracts (EAA)*, Sage Publications, Inc., 2455 Teller Road, Newbury Park, CA 91320

- *IBZ International Bibliography of Periodical Literature,* Zeller Verlag GmbH & Co., P.O. Box 1949, d-49009 Osnabruck, Germany

- *Index to Periodical Articles Related to Law*, University of Texas, 727 East 26th Street, Austin, TX 78705

- *Information Reports & Bibliographies*, Science Associates International, Inc., 6 Hastings Road, Marlboro, NJ 07746-1313

- *Information Science Abstracts*, Plenum Publishing Company, 233 Spring Street, New York, NY 10013-1578

- *Informed Librarian, The,* Infosources Publishing, 140 Norma Road, Teaneck, NJ 07666

- *INSPEC Information Services,* Institution of Electrical Engineers, Michael Faraday House, Six Hills Way, Stevenage, Herts SG1 2AY, England

(continued)

- *INTERNET ACCESS (& additional networks) Bulletin Board for Libraries ("BUBL"), coverage of information resources on INTERNET, JANET, and other networks.*
    - <URL:http://bubl.ac.uk/>
    - The new locations will be found under <URL:http://bubl.ac.uk/link/>.
    - Any existing BUBL users who have problems finding information on the new service should contact the BUBL help line by sending e-mail to <bubl@bubl.ac.uk>.

  The Andersonian Library, Curran Building, 101 St. James Road, Glasgow G4 0NS, Scotland

- *Journal of Academic Librarianship: Guide to Professional Literature, The,* Graduate School of Library & Information Science/Simmons College, 300 The Fenway, Boston, MA 02115-5898

- *Library & Information Science Abstracts (LISA),* Bowker-Saur Limited, Maypole House, Maypole Road, East Grinstead, West Sussex RH19 1HH, England

- *Library and Information Science Annual (LISCA),* Libraries Unlimited, PO Box 6633, Englewood, CO 80155-6633. Further information is available at www.lu.com/arba

- *Library Literature,* The H.W. Wilson Company, 950 University Avenue, Bronx, NY 10452

- *National Clearinghouse on Child Abuse & Neglect,* 10530 Rosehaven Street, Suite 400, Fairfax, VA 22030-2804

- *Newsletter of Library and Information Services*, China Sci-Tech Book Review, Library of Academia Sinica, 8 Kexueyuan Nanlu, Zhongguancun, Beijing 100080, People's Republic of China

- *NIAAA Alcohol and Alcohol Problems Science Database (ETOH),* National Institute on Alcohol Abuse and Alcoholism Science Database, 1400 Eye Street NW, Suite 200, Washington, DC 20005

- *PASCAL,* % Institute de L'Information Scientifique et Technique. Cross-disciplinary electronic database covering the fields of science, technology & medicine. Also available on CD-ROM, and can generate customized retrospective searches. For more information: INIST, Customer Desk, 2, allee du Parc de Brabois, F-54514 Vandoeuvre Cedex, France (http//www.inist.fr), INIST/CNRS-Service Gestion des Documents Primaires, 2, allee du Parc de Brabois, F-54514 Vandoeuvre-les-Nancy, Cedex, France

- *REHABDATA, National Rehabilitation Information Center (NARIC),* Searches are available in large-print, cassette or Braille format and all are available on PC-compatible diskette. Also accessible via the Internet at http//www.naric.com/naric. 8455 Colesville Road, Suite 935, Silver Spring, MD 20910-3319

(continued)

SPECIAL BIBLIOGRAPHIC NOTES

related to special journal issues (separates)
and indexing/abstracting

☐ indexing/abstracting services in this list will also cover material in any "separate" that is co-published simultaneously with Haworth's special thematic journal issue or DocuSerial. Indexing/abstracting usually covers material at the article/chapter level.

☐ monographic co-editions are intended for either non-subscribers or libraries which intend to purchase a second copy for their circulating collections.

☐ monographic co-editions are reported to all jobbers/wholesalers/approval plans. The source journal is listed as the "series" to assist the prevention of duplicate purchasing in the same manner utilized for books-in-series.

☐ to facilitate user/access services all indexing/abstracting services are encouraged to utilize the co-indexing entry note indicated at the bottom of the first page of each article/chapter/contribution.

☐ this is intended to assist a library user of any reference tool (whether print, electronic, online, or CD-ROM) to locate the monographic version if the library has purchased this version but not a subscription to the source journal.

☐ individual articles/chapters in any Haworth publication are also available through the Haworth Document Delivery Service (HDDS).

Public Library Collection Development in the Information Age

CONTENTS

ABOUT THE EDITOR

Annabel K. Stephens is Associate Professor at the University of Alabama's School of Library and Information Studies, where she has taught classes in collection development, public libraries, and adult materials and services for twelve years. Previously, Dr. Stephens worked in the public libraries of Alabama, Mississippi and Tennessee. She has published numerous articles on public library planning and is the author of *Assessing the Public Library Planning Process,* published in 1995.

Introduction

Annabel K. Stephens

This volume's title was chosen to describe the climate within which librarians are striving to develop collections for today's public libraries. Within our profession, these waning years of the twentieth century are constantly referred to in speeches and in print as the "Age of Information," in reference to both the exponential growth in print and electronic information resources, and the increasing interest in and use of those resources by public library patrons. Patrons are coming to public libraries in ever-growing numbers, and many of them are also accessing information from their homes via computer. During this "information age," librarians, also, are increasing their reliance on information in both print and electronic form to facilitate their work, including the building and maintaining of public library collections.

Librarians are evaluating, selecting, and accessing more and more information resources today than ever before. They are also using ever-increasing amounts of information in every aspect of collection development work. Increasing uses of technology and excitement as collection developers discover the benefits of using the Internet in their work are also characteristic of our times. Each of these themes is explored by the authors included in this collection, and their articles, taken together, illustrate many of the trends and issues involved in information age public library collection development.

Articles by Thorsen, Stephens, and Waznis illustrate libraries' uses of information in planning and budgeting for collection development. Thorsen's King County (Washington) Library System has conducted community studies of many of its diverse service areas for use in planning local

[Haworth co-indexing entry note]: "Introduction." Stephens, Annabel K. Co-published simultaneously in *The Acquisitions Librarian* (The Haworth Press, Inc.) No. 20, 1998, pp. 1-3; and: *Public Library Collection Development in the Information Age* (ed: Annabel K. Stephens) The Haworth Press, Inc., 1998, pp. 1-3. Single or multiple copies of this article are available for a fee from The Haworth Document Delivery Service [1-800-342-9678, 9:00 a.m. - 5:00 p.m. (EST). E-mail address: getinfo@ haworthpressinc.com].

1

services and collections. She describes the process used, the types of information studied, and the recommendations of some of the studies. Stephens examines the impact on collection development of the information collected and decisions made during over 255 libraries' use of the public library planning process. Waznis's San Diego County Library System has developed a method that considers population impact, property tax revenues, circulation, reference needs, and special children's and outreach projects, among other factors, in allocating book budget funds. She describes both the overall process and the rationale behind the factors considered.

Articles by Gibson, Lee, and Davis inform us about three relatively new directions that many of today's public library collection developers are taking or considering: centralized selection, jobber-assisted selection, and the conspectus approach for collection evaluation. Selection at Gibson's Indianapolis-Marion County Library has been centralized for five years, and she explains the why and how and the benefits involved. Attention is paid to branch demographics and use and to patron requests; branch librarians have input into the process; and future plans include "paperless selection" and electronic ordering. Lee's article describes the "local" and "global" information needed for making good selection decisions, the importance of good communication between selector and vendor, and the five levels of assistance provided to selectors by the Brodart Company. Davis discusses benefits of using the WLN Conspectus to assess small public libraries' collections. She explains types of information needed for assessment and suggests techniques and adaptations for small libraries.

The next set of articles, by Greiner, Guarino, Milnor, Poisson, and Hastings, focus on technology, the Internet, and other electronic resources. Both their impact on the collection development process and on the content of libraries' collections are explored.

Greiner visited and interviewed directors and selected staff of two libraries in England and one in Scotland, and she writes about the effect of technology on their collection development policies and practices. Needs assessment efforts and censorship practices of these libraries are also described. Guarino provides advice on integrating the Internet into both a library's collection development process and its daily operations. She emphasizes the importance of acceptable use policies, rules and regulations for Internet access, and providing staff with technical training and help with finding, evaluating, and knowing when to use Internet resources. Based on interviews with "working librarians," who use the Internet for selection and acquisitions and for keeping apprised of new and current topics, Milnor's article also comments on its impact on both purchasing decisions and money available for print and audio visual resources. Poisson describes the process used for selection and implementation of electronic resources at New York Public Library's Science, Industry and Business Library (SIBL). Hastings outlines criteria for selecting and methods of evaluating networked resources (networked CD-ROMs and resources included on Web sites).

Christenson, Gough and Greenblatt, and Watson provide information and advice for selectors of both electronic and print resources. Christenson's resource list for rural and small town libraries includes citations to numerous Internet web sites, catalogs and bibliographies, and publishers and other relevant agencies and organizations. Gough and Greenblatt provide extensive help for selectors of materials for gay and lesbian patrons. Print and Internet sources of bibliographic data, reviews, and best-seller and award lists are included along with suggestions of topics to cover and a checklist of questions and reminders for selectors. Watson reviews traditional strategies used for identifying and evaluating multicultural children's literature and proposes integrating web sites into the process; many useful sites are listed and annotated.

Formal library and information science education and staff development for collection development are the topics of the closing articles. Gregory includes the topics explored in her Collection Development course at the University of South Florida where she attempts to prepare students for the problems created by emphasis on electronic formats, while Elliott relates the Public Library of Nashville and Davidson County's efforts to prepare its staff for developing collections in the midst of technological and other changes.

From planning and budgeting, to exploring new methods and resources for building and evaluating collections, to education and training for improved collection development—the articles in this volume illustrate and emphasize the importance and use of information and information technologies in our current collection development efforts. The articles also contain much valuable information and many practical and helpful suggestions for today's librarians and those who will be building collections for the public library patrons of the next century.

Community Studies:
Raising the Roof
and Other Recommendations

Jeanne Thorsen

SUMMARY. King County Library System serves over a million people within two thousand square miles. Profiles of library service areas provide an avenue to gather data on local areas and to gauge a library's connection to its community. This article describes the community study process, including data gathering, conclusions and recommendations. Profiles of recent studies and recommendations for collections, programs, and services are included. *[Article copies available for a fee from The Haworth Document Delivery Service: 1-800-342-9678. E-mail address: getinfo@haworthpressinc.com]*

Imagine you've just flown in from Jupiter and your assignment is to study a library service area and make recommendations for improved services. That's exactly the starting point for the community studies conducted by the King County Library System. The emphasis is on a fresh new look at each area and the result is a package of recommendations for enhanced services and collections.

Located in western Washington state, King County Library System (KCLS) pays attention to the unique characteristics of forty library service

Jeanne Thorsen is Manager of Community Relations for King County Library System and coordinator of more than twenty community studies. For more information, or samples of studies, contact the KCLS Community Relations Office, 300 8th Avenue North, Seattle, WA 98109.

[Haworth co-indexing entry note]: "Community Studies: Raising the Roof and Other Recommendations." Thorsen, Jeanne. Co-published simultaneously in *The Acquisitions Librarian* (The Haworth Press, Inc.) No. 20, 1998, pp. 5-13; and: *Public Library Collection Development in the Information Age* (ed: Annabel K. Stephens) The Haworth Press, Inc., 1998, pp. 5-13. Single or multiple copies of this article are available for a fee from The Haworth Document Delivery Service [1-800-342-9678, 9:00 a.m. - 5:00 p.m. (EST). E-mail address: getinfo@haworthpressinc.com].

areas–community by community, study by study. KCLS serves over one million people within 2,200 square miles–in cities, suburbs, ex-urbs, and rural zones.

A decade ago, population projections, collection distribution statistics, and role assignments for each branch laid the groundwork for a successful $67 million bond issue for new buildings and materials. At that time, some areas of the county were unserved, others underserved. In 1990, the Library System began its ambitious building program that will construct twenty new facilities by the year 2002.

While the system-wide data were useful, insight on local communities and their information needs was lacking. So, these studies were designed to elicit this information, create expectations on how local libraries could connect with their communities, and provide a means for these libraries to gauge their success. Since 1991, twenty-four of these service needs assessments have been completed. Each one focuses on a library branch and its identified service area, each has conclusions and recommendations, and each establishes standards for local service.

The study process provides an opportunity to focus time and attention on a particular branch and community. An in-depth look at each library service area reveals demographic information, along with neighborhood profiles, community concerns, growth patterns, business plans, social and recreational services, and educational issues; in short, a description of a community's personality. With this information, it is possible to continue the system-wide distribution of collections and services while also providing an overlay of special collections and services tailor-made for each service area.

This article will describe the community study process, discuss areas of research, and present a sampling of recommendations.

IN THE BEGINNING

Each fall the Public Services Associate Directors decide the four libraries to be studied the following year. Service area boundaries are based on major roads, city boundaries or geographical features. It is ideal when these boundaries fall neatly along the census tract lines. For a variety of reasons, including common sense, tracts are sometimes split with another library's service area. It is also understood that these boundaries are artificial; people use libraries near where they live, and stop at branches that are close to soccer games, stores, and work.

Each study includes a team of subject experts and managers who specialize in particular areas: Government Documents Librarian–census data, demographic information; Business Librarian–zoning, growth, commute times; Traveling Library Center Manager–outreach, senior services, social services, recreation; Children's Services Coordinator–child care, education issues; Young Adult and Literacy Coordinator–youth and education issues, literacy, post-secondary schools; Branch Manager–history of the area, library history; Public Services Associate Director responsible for the branch–geography, transportation, civic issues; plus the Library System Director and a representative from the Collection Management Services division participate in the conclusions and recommendations phase of the project.

The study schedule and process is guided by the Manager of Community Relations. Editing, maps and report compilation is coordinated by a Public Services Division Assistant. Each study comprises approximately five meetings of the study team, plus hours of data collection, review and analysis.

The introduction of a new area and the Branch Manager's participation ensures originality and keen interest in each project.

GETTING TO KNOW YOU

To get started, the entire team goes on a two-hour "drive-around" of the area, with a travelogue provided by the Branch Manager. The drive-around is like a Polaroid snapshot–at first, when everyone gets in the van, the image of the community is rather blurry, yet as more miles and time pass, the picture comes into focus.

The drive-around also provides an opportunity to take a fresh new look at the community. The tour includes schools, major businesses, natural boundaries, neighborhoods, new developments, parks, community centers, etc., and at least one coffee stop. The goal is for everyone on the team to be visually aware of the service area so that later when someone refers to "the new developments on the ridge" or "the annual flooding," everyone on the team instantly recognizes the locale.

Another activity that takes place during the drive-around is the naming of the census tracts. Neighborhood names are attached to the tract numbers for ease of identification.

GETTING TO KNOW ALL ABOUT YOU

Numerous sources are used to compile the data for the study, including maps, comprehensive plans, local history documents, school projections, interviews with city, school district and agency officials, and other resources. Census information often proves to be a problem; much of it is out of date, particularly in the area of ethnic populations. Local projections, marketing studies, and school district data on languages spoken and free lunches provided offer supplementary information.

Once the sections are written and assembled into the first draft of the report, the study team meets to discuss the findings. Each chapter is reviewed, issues are addressed, and new questions and areas to research often emerge. And, every once in awhile, there is an "aha"–a question or issue so on point that the focus of the study takes on new clarity. After the initial discussion, group members scurry off with new assignments, then regroup in a couple of weeks to present updated information.

COMING TO CONCLUSIONS

The ground rules for including an idea in the conclusions and/or recommendations are simple:

1. It must be in the findings in the report before it can be cited as a conclusion.
2. It must be listed in the conclusions section before it can be listed as a recommendation.
3. If a recommendation is a really good idea but it is not in the report, it is worthwhile to go back to 1. and 2.

Conclusions are drawn about the community; no conclusions are included about current library services. During this phase, the team clarifies its description of the community and the key issues involved. This discussion is so vital that it often takes two meetings to complete.

RAISING THE ROOF AND OTHER RECOMMENDATIONS

In response to the conclusions drawn, the team develops library service recommendations. Coming up with creative solutions that address community needs within current budget allocations is a challenge. Brainstorming is common. The Branch Manager has an opportunity to participate in, to show leadership in, planning that includes changes in certain services–over time. The twenty to thirty recommendations are intended to be phased in over a period of years. The schedule to implement the various recommendations is determined during annual goal-setting sessions.

While the intent is to make recommendations within the current staffing and budget allocations, every once in awhile the results of a study clearly show a need for more staffing, or even for a new building.

Here are some examples from recent studies.

Kent is a city of sixty-four thousand residents and is a manufacturing center in south King County; the Boeing Company is one of the major employers. There have been dramatic demographic and economic changes in the last decade: increases in population, housing stock (more apartments and condominiums), and renter occupancy and mobility. The Kent Regional Library (twenty-two thousand square feet) serves the community. Recommendations include:

- Develop a marketing plan to reach the thousands of residents in rent-subsidized apartments near the Library; provide information about Library services to children and families.
- Co-sponsor series on parenting, with social service organizations in the area.
- Focus government documents collection on defense and aerospace industries, including surveys and maps, NASA documents, etc.

Called the "Carmel of the North," Kirkland is an arts-oriented community on the shore of Lake Washington. Its waterfront orientation and variety of businesses makes it a popular destination for residents, shoppers, walkers, and diners. Residents for the most part are young, educated, employed in administrative positions, and have incomes higher than the county average. A fifteen thousand square foot library in conjunction with a city parking garage opened in 1995. Recommendations include:

- Incorporate art and art events into the structure and activities of the Library. Create an outdoor sculpture garden to accommodate changing exhibits; feature work by glass artists and sculptors inside the Library.
- Coordinate efforts with the city and organizations for inclusion of the Library in arts celebrations, and in the monthly "art walk" events.

Burien is an area in transition from a long-established residential community to a new city with thirty thousand residents. The Library service area includes quiet, single-family neighborhoods, multi-family housing on major arterials, residents of a variety of ages and income and education levels, and a business section that seeks revitalization. There is a large number of youth, though not much for them to do in the way of recreation.

The Burien Library was recently expanded to twenty thousand square feet to serve this growing–and changing–area. Recommendations include:

- Extend open hours on Friday evenings until midnight; create a program for teens in the meeting room while serving patrons of all ages in the Library.
- Hold family-based programs on nights and weekends to accommodate single and working parents.
- Evaluate and enhance the collection to ensure representation of interests and concerns of a growing multi-ethnic population.

The small town of Snoqualmie (population fifteen hundred) will undergo major change when a planned development will bring in twenty-five hundred homes and ten thousand people by the year 2000. Snoqualmie is located in a scenic, semi-isolated valley near the top of Snoqualmie Pass. The historical part of town is located in an area that floods frequently, thus growth is limited; the new homes will be on the ridge. The popular five thousand square foot Snoqualmie Library serves the community. Recommendations include:

- Create an information center in the Library that includes materials about the community, including its logging and railroad history. Based on history, expand the collection of railroad books.
- Work with local historical organizations and businesses to provide access to historical information through collections, electronic access, and public programming.
- Explore ways for the Library to become a bridging agency that unites current and new residents.
- Within five years, launch a planning process for library services; explore possibility of a new, larger library building.

Mercer Island is situated in the middle of Lake Washington one mile east of Seattle and just west of Bellevue. Since the 1950s, it has been home to the most influential movers and shakers in the area. The island is known for its quality of life and quality of education. Residents are graying: the median age is older than the rest of the county, and the number of school children is significantly lower than in past years. The fifteen thousand square foot Mercer Island Library serves the twenty-one thousand residents. Recommendations include:

- Focus business collection on titles for investors, entrepreneurs, and home-based businesses.

- Expand materials for college-bound students, including college catalogs.
- The island has the largest Jewish community in the state; increase holdings on the history of the Middle East, travel in the Middle East, and the Holocaust.
- House 'patron request' materials (a variety of special titles ordered throughout the system) in this branch.

Boulevard Park is an unincorporated area just south of the Seattle city limits. A once-thriving business and residential community, the area now consists mostly of small businesses and lower-value homes (due to nearby airport noise). Residents have lower levels of educational attainment though higher income levels when compared to the rest of the county. The five thousand square foot Boulevard Park Library is a popular place for all ages. Recommendations include:

- Increase awareness of nearby social service agencies; provide information and referral.
- Establish a "Personal Discovery Center" section in the Library that includes career information, job finding materials, employment directories, vocational test books, etc.

Federal Way is a city of contrasts and changes. In the southwest corner of King County, Federal Way offers plentiful affordable housing and commercial opportunities. These factors also inhibit its ability to form a sense of community. There are nearly one hundred thousand residents, and one-third are under age eighteen. Federal Way also is one of the most diverse communities in the county in terms of ethnicity and immigrant groups. The Federal Way 320th Library (ten thousand square feet) has served the community for 20 years; the Federal Way Regional Library (twenty-five thousand square feet) opened in 1991. Recommendations include:

- Explore evening and weekend story times and programs to better meet the needs of single and working parents. Establish connections with Korean Chamber of Commerce and Korean business community.
- Expand and promote Korean collections; explore scheduling a Korean story time for children.
- Develop information for businesses considering relocation to the area; highlight library resources.
- Promote the libraries as institutions that strongly identify with Federal Way and that are vital to residents' information needs and integral to the community's quality of life.

THE STUDY COMES TO LIFE

During the tenure of the study, there are often three drafts of the report: the first draft is the compilation of the sections, the second draft includes updated information and is ready just prior to the conclusions and recommendations discussions, and the final draft is reviewed prior to publication.

The last official act of the team is the presentation of the findings to the KCLS Board of Trustees. One way that the Board members stay in touch with the communities served is to hold its meetings in the various branches. Each year, the Board takes its meetings to the four libraries studied. Highlights of the study are presented through maps, slides, statistics, and summaries of the topical areas.

One hundred copies of the report are produced. Copies are sent to each Library Manager and Department Manager in the System, to each Board member; additional copies are provided to the library studied for local board members or city officials.

What has been described here is an orderly, cohesive, linear process that reflects reality most of the time. Each study takes on a personality all its own. There are sometimes disruptions, disagreements, and detours along the way which are beneficial because additional information is unearthed, new opinions are considered, and creative ideas are acknowledged. These ideas bring life to the description of the community studied, and to the final document.

CONCLUSION

Community studies provide an opportunity for this large organization to stay in touch with the communities it serves. While the majority of services are delivered in a system-wide fashion, this process provides an avenue by which to tailor collections, programs, and outreach activities to unique areas of the county.

What is important is that attention is focused on the communities and changes are made in the delivery of services to reflect the needs of those who use the Library. It is also important that the information gleaned and presented in the studies correctly describes the community. There are a number of organizations in the region who study population patterns, economic forecasts, and social needs. But the Library System may be the only agency that studies these communities with the goal of providing improved service.

Though it may seem silly to pretend that we're from Jupiter in order to exercise objectivity for the study, it helps us to focus our research on each new area we visit. One of our study teams recently presented its findings to the Board of Trustees at one of the community libraries. One resident who attended said that not only did the team "get it right," she added that the study team "got it better than anyone else." That's high praise, and it makes the study, including the drive-around, the discussions, and even the detours worth all the effort.

The Public Library Planning Process: Its Impact on Collection Development Policies and Practices

Annabel K. Stephens

SUMMARY. Public libraries have derived numerous benefits from their use of the PLA planning process. Many libraries have used the process to improve their collection development policies and practices and to make fundamental changes in their collection's focus and content. This article reports on the process's impact on collection development at more than 255 libraries. *[Article copies available for a fee from The Haworth Document Delivery Service: 1-800-342-9678. E-mail address: getinfo@haworthpressinc.com]*

INTRODUCTION

In 1980 the American Library Association published what was then a revolutionary new tool to encourage and assist public librarians in community-based comprehensive planning. *A Planning Process for Public Libraries*[1] introduced a process to help librarians, along with trustees and other community members, collect and assess information on the library/

Annabel K. Stephens is Associate Professor at the School of Library and Information Studies, University of Alabama, P.O. Box 870252, Tuscaloosa, AL 35487-0252.

Portions of this article were previously published in *Assessing the Public Library Planning Process*. Norwood, NJ: Ablex Publishing Company, 1994.

[Haworth co-indexing entry note]: "The Public Library Planning Process: Its Impact on Collection Development Policies and Practices." Stephens, Annabel K. Co-published simultaneously in *The Acquisitions Librarian* (The Haworth Press, Inc.) No. 20, 1998, pp. 15-23; and: *Public Library Collection Development in the Information Age* (ed: Annabel K. Stephens) The Haworth Press, Inc., 1998, pp. 15-23. Single or multiple copies of this article are available for a fee from The Haworth Document Delivery Service [1-800-342-9678, 9:00 a.m. - 5:00 p.m. (EST). E-mail address: getinfo@haworthpressinc.com].

information needs of local communities and plan collections and services relevant to community needs. The manual containing this process was revised and expanded and published in 1987 as *Planning and Role Setting for Public Libraries: A Manual of Options and Procedures*.[2]

Because little was known about the actual impact on the thousands of libraries across the country that had adopted the planning process, the author conducted a study[3] of the use of *Planning and Role Setting for Public Libraries* in 1991. Based on the planning experiences of over 255 libraries, this article reports what was discovered about the process's impact on these libraries' collection development policies and practices.

THE PLANNING PROCESS

The process outlined in *Planning and Role Setting for Public Libraries* . . . includes a community analysis step ("looking around") during which librarians select information from the census and other published reports, interview community members, conduct user and community surveys, and perform output measures. They use the information obtained during this step in choosing from a menu of possible roles for the libraries to emphasize for the next several years.

The planning manual includes examples of specific types of materials that libraries should offer for each of the roles[4] described. Popular Materials Library, Preschoolers' Door to Learning, and Reference Library have been the roles chosen by the majority of libraries. The Popular Materials Library role calls for collecting "current and popular materials in a variety of formats, with sufficient duplication to meet demand." A substantial percentage of these materials are to have been published within the last five years.[5] The Preschoolers' Door to Learning role encourages inclusion of a "variety of materials and formats for preschoolers and for adults working with young children, . . . computers, audiovisual formats, educational toys, and games to help children expand their imagination and develop motor and sensory skills," and multiple copies of popular titles.[6] Libraries choosing the Reference Library role "emphasize informational materials to support individual, business, government and community interests," with materials for all ages and reading levels. The "extensive" reference collection in these libraries "includes such material as indexes, atlases, encyclopedias, handbooks, and directories," "makes heavy use of electronic databases," and "has a large current periodicals collection." The libraries may subscribe to "special indexing and abstracting services and keep files on area businesses" and may also emphasize "development of local history archives and collecting local documents, memorabilia, and photographs."[7]

The Community Information Center role calls for the collection to contain "locally developed files of information on community agencies, clubs, and interest groups, vertical files on issues of current interest, local newspapers and newsletters of local agencies and organizations, on-line services."[8] The Formal Education Support Center role necessitates "materials in all formats and at levels appropriate to the educational levels supported by the library–reference materials, periodicals, abstracting and indexing services, on-line databases, and access to interlibrary loan," including "materials listed as supplemental sources in textbooks used by local education providers."[9] Libraries choosing the Independent Learning Center role will have a "wide range of circulating subject materials relevant to the interests of independent learners of all ages in a variety of formats and geared to varying levels of ability." Some will develop "extensive collections of audio or video cassettes on popular self-help topics such as health issues, investment planning, home planning, foreign languages, and psychology."[10]

PROCESS'S IMPACT ON COLLECTION DEVELOPMENT: PUBLISHED REPORTS

A few examples of the process's impact on collection development had been reported in the literature prior to the author's study. The former director of Georgia's Pine Mountain Regional Library[11] listed greater attention paid to collection development and evaluation and a 91 percent increase in local funding among the several benefits attributed to her library's planning process.

The Crawford Memorial Library in Monticello, New York, made several specific changes in development and promotion of its collection based on its choice of roles. Weeding, use of materials dumps and other merchandising techniques, shifting books from reference to circulation, renting popular titles, increasing paperbacks and multiple copies of best sellers were initiated in support of its Popular Materials role. Fifty percent of the materials budget for children was designated as a strategy for its role of Children's Door to Learning.[12]

Verna Pungitore[13] (Indiana University) listed the many benefits achieved by the libraries whose planning experiences she studied. Pungitore wrote that the process generated information on perceptions and information needs of users and nonusers and guided decisions concerning materials and services. Examples of specific results affecting collection development were decisions to weed parts of collections and deemphasize various roles not chosen as primary.

LIBRARIES IN 1991 STUDY

In 1991 the author surveyed over a thousand librarians in forty-four states and eight provinces about their use of the 1987 planning and role setting manual.[14] Replies were received from 303 libraries, but only 255 were usable.[15] These 255 libraries are in thirty-two states and two provinces. Seventy-four serve less than 10,000 people, sixty-six serve more than 100,000, and one-hundred and fifteen serve between 10,000 and 100,000. The average population served is 26,673. The majority (59%) are single libraries without branches; 36 percent are systems with branches and one board; and 3 percent are federated systems (systems with member libraries that have their own boards).

The librarians in the 1991 study used the planning process to create and revise their collection development policies and practices; to increase attention paid to weeding, collection assessment, and cooperative collection development; and to make fundamental changes in the types and formats of materials included in their collections. The extent of their changes in materials collected and the illustrative comments supplied by many of the librarians provide strong evidence that both the information collected during the "looking around" phase and the roles chosen to address the community needs discovered were vital to these decisions.

Policies and Plans/Procedures and Practices

Several librarians credited the process with increasing emphasis on the collection development process and with influencing creation or refocusing of collection development policies and plans. These acknowledged: "[I] [r]ealized how few written policies we had"; "We wrote policies and procedures for the first time!"; "We now have policies—when we never did before." A librarian commented that one of his "major objectives" had been "development of a collection development statement and better allocation of the materials budget," while a second was "currently producing a collection development plan that will result in changed emphasis." Others wrote: "The planning process has increased awareness and initiated better decision-making"; "We've set some priorities. I hadn't really prioritized before"; and "We had no direction and now we know where we are going."

It was very apparent from the comments that in many of the libraries development and revision of policies had led to specific changes in collection development procedures and practices. Librarians centralized collection development efforts, began buying reference materials on a regional rather than a branch-by-branch basis, and revised purchasing procedures for adding and expanding collections in specific areas. Others decided to emphasize pre-publication ordering when possible, allow purchase of more "best-sellers" regardless of reviews, and increase emphasis on multiple copies and "quality as perceived by the customer."

Librarians began purchasing requested materials rather than relying on interlibrary loan; negotiated cooperative collection development agreements with university, community college, and special libraries; devoted greater attention to patrons' requests; and developed clearer selection criteria and easier budgeting formulae. Others reported they had become more aware of the importance of weeding and better able to write collection management policies and assess their collections.

Changes in Formats and Types of Material

One-hundred and thirty-six of the librarians (68 percent of those answering) reported that they had added, dropped, or changed emphasis on collecting certain types of materials or formats as a result of their use of the planning process. Many of these provided examples. Most changes involved increased emphasis on popular materials, reference materials, or materials for children and students of all ages, or the addition, deletion, increase, or decrease of certain categories of audio-visual materials.

Thirty-nine librarians had increased emphasis on popular materials including more purchases of paperbacks and multiple copies of current materials. Thirteen had increased emphasis on reference materials, including periodicals, while three had decreased their emphasis. Sixteen librarians reported an increased emphasis on children's materials and two an increased emphasis on materials for young adults. A few reported increased emphasis on student-related materials and literacy materials.

Other changes included addition or increased emphasis on large-print materials, self-teaching or self-improvement materials, career and educational guidance materials, and black interest and parenting materials. Four libraries had added computer databases, and two had begun collections of educational software.

Ten librarians wrote that they were placing more emphasis on audio-visual materials, but did not specify particular formats. Others reported adding or increasing emphasis on compact discs and audio, music, and videocassettes. A few had discontinued their collections of phonograph records, films, filmstrips, slides, and framed reproductions, while two reported placing less emphasis on videocassettes.

Use of "Looking Around" Information

In gathering information about the library and its community, 83 percent of the libraries had used printed sources and library materials, 57 percent had conducted interviews and surveys, and 63 percent had calculated output measures. Many of the librarians indicated that the information collected while "looking around" had greatly influenced their collection development decisions. Based on demographics studied during this phase, one library had increased the percentage of funds for children's materials and materials in Spanish. Others had "added materials according to patrons' requests that we weren't aware of" and had "extensively studied circulation to determine the most popular materials and reallocated our budget accordingly." The importance of survey information was specifically acknowledged by those who wrote: "Through our Telephone Survey, we found out what patrons really would like to see in our library"; "Our survey told us usage [in regard to] records, cassettes and CDs"; and "Book buying patterns were greatly influenced by the survey feedback."

Impact of Role Selection Process

The vast majority of the study libraries had used the role selection step outlined by the process. Eighty-eight percent had chosen roles from those listed in the planning and role setting manual; 48 percent had adapted the manual's roles or chosen others; 35 percent had done both. Listed in order of popularity, Popular Materials Center, Preschoolers' Door to Learning, Reference Library, Formal Education Support Center, and Independent Learning Center were the roles chosen by over half of the librarians that reported their choices. Several commented that their collection development policies and practices had been powerfully influenced by the process of role selection:

- "[We] have focused collection development to roles";
- "We changed statements in the selection policy to fit our roles";
- "We are able to prioritize services and materials based on the roles identified in the plan";
- "Roles have had a definite impact on our collection development; this has been the most important area";
- "By defining each branch's roles, we have drafted a collection development plan for a collection to meet that role"; and

• "The selection of roles will ultimately probably have the most significance in that it will directly impact the way in which materials budgets are allocated. This process is causing staff to consider why we make the collection development decisions we make–what is our intent and what role does it support."

Librarians wrote that choosing specific roles for their libraries to emphasize had legitimized developing parts of the collection while deemphasizing others: "Emphasis is not as much on historical and/or archival materials since we know our mission"; "Selecting roles allowed us to narrow our focus rather than 'being all things to all patrons.' We [now] select more heavily in popular fiction and children's materials and less in reference and business"; and "As a result of choosing roles, it has been easier to make acquisitions and weeding decisions; we no longer need to try to be all things to all people." The sometimes-forgotten concept that role selection is to be repeated over time was illustrated by a director who explained, "In our first planning year we identified Preschoolers' Door to Learning as our 2nd role and with this in mind allocated [the] materials budget accordingly. In the 3rd year of planning this role was moved downward."

Links Between Roles and Choices

Several librarians offered specific examples of how particular roles were linked with their particular collection development decisions. Libraries that chose the role of Formal Education Support Center had added CD-ROM reference materials, placed more emphasis on obtaining materials corresponding with school assignments and curriculum, and moved "toward purchase of more juvenile materials and realization of [our] role in supplementing K-12 school assignments–never articulated before." Conversely, a librarian who had chosen not to emphasize this role reported that "clarification of [our] role has underscored [the] need to strengthen local school libraries so public libraries can move beyond [a] default role and strengthen our own mission statement."

One librarian had reallocated more funds to reference sources because Reference Library was chosen as her library's main role. Others reported adding more children's books to fit the role of Preschoolers' Door to Learning and emphasizing popular materials at branch libraries and increasing purchase of video and compact discs because of their Popular Materials Library role.

CONCLUSION

The potential of the public library planning process to influence collection development policies, procedures, and decisions was well-illustrated by the many study libraries that had established or revised their collection development policies and procedures and/or made far-reaching changes in their collections' focus and in the types and formats of materials acquired. Many of the librarians' comments provided strong evidence that the information collected during "looking around" and the roles selected during the "developing roles and mission" step had been especially helpful and had, in many cases, been used to bring about the changes reported. Perhaps the value of the planning process to collection development can best be summarized by the comments of two study respondents who acknowledged this potential. One wrote, "I can look at it two ways: (1) I'm full of this information or have access to it and can't use it fast enough. Frustration! (2) At least I have options and don't have to continue just 'as we've always done.' " The other director explained that last time his system "did not do an extensive collection assessment, feeling that the individual libraries should be emphasizing this. They didn't. They will this time!"

REFERENCES

1. Vernon E. Palmour, Marcia Bellasai, and Nancy DeWath. *A Planning Process for Public Libraries*. Chicago: American Library Association, 1980.

2. Charles E. McClure, Douglas L. Zweizig, Mary Jo Lynch, and Nancy Van House. *Planning and Role Setting for Public Libraries: A Manual of Options and Procedures*. Chicago: American Library Association, 1987.

3. Annabel K. Stephens. *Assessing the Public Library Planning Process*. Norwood, NJ: Ablex, 1995.

4. The new manual scheduled for publication in late 1997 or early 1998 suggests the use of "service responses" rather than roles. Basic Literacy, Business & Career Information, Catalyst, Commons, Community Referral, Consumer Information, General Information, Government Information, Information Literacy, Lifelong Learning, Local History & Genealogy, Cultural Awareness, Current Topics & Titles, Formal Learning Support are among those being considered.

5. *Planning and Role Setting for Public Libraries* . . . , p. 36.

6. *Planning and Role Setting for Public Libraries* . . . , p. 37.

7. *Planning and Role Setting for Public Libraries* . . . , pp. 38-39.

8. *Planning and Role Setting for Public Libraries* . . . , p. 33.

9. *Planning and Role Setting for Public Libraries* . . . , p. 34.

10. *Planning and Role Setting for Public Libraries* . . . , p. 35.

11. Lyn Hopper, "Planning Pays for the Small, the Poor, and the Busy: An Exhortation and a Bibliography," *Public Libraries* 30 (January/February, 1991): 21-24.

12. Allen Barrish and Dennis Carrigan, "Strategic Planning and the Small Public Library: A Case Study," *Public Libraries* 30 (September/October, 1991): 283-287.

13. Verna Pungitore, "The Public Library Planning Process: Case Studies of Its Implementation in Smaller Libraries" (Final Report) Bloomington: Indiana University School of Library and Information Science, 1991.

14. Included all libraries with roles listed in the *Public Library Data Service Statistical Report* from 1988 through 1991 and libraries nominated by their state or provincial library agencies as then using or having used the planning process since 1987.

15. Nine librarians with roles in the . . . *Statistical Report* wrote that they had not used the planning manual, as did twenty-nine librarians nominated by their state and provincial library agencies. Others wrote that their predecessors had left little documentation.

Materials Budget Allocation Methods at San Diego County Library

Betty Waznis

SUMMARY. Methods used to allocate the materials budget at San Diego County Library, California, are discussed. The San Diego County Library is a large and diverse conglomeration of small-town, rural, and suburban libraries with below-average funding. With a per capita materials budget of only 93 cents, the method of allocating the book budget is something that is closely watched by library Friends groups, city governments, and community organizations. The staff first takes into account the portion of the entire library budget devoted to materials, and core service levels and reference needs at individual branches. The components of the materials budget are "base" budgets, service-measurement allocations, and centralized expenditures, all of which are examined and adjusted each year. The library attempts to balance these factors with the public and staff perception of what is "fair," together with a method of allocation that will satisfy the service goals of the organization. *[Article copies available for a fee from The Haworth Document Delivery Service: 1-800-342-9678. E-mail address: getinfo@haworthpressinc.com]*

San Diego County Library is one of eight library jurisdictions in San Diego County, California. It serves a population of about 901,000 in 11 incorporated cities and the unincorporated area of the county. San Diego County also includes seven other public libraries run by municipalities:

Betty Waznis is Collection Development Librarian, San Diego County Library, Bldg. 15, 5555 Overland Avenue, San Diego, CA 92123-1296.

[Haworth co-indexing entry note]: "Materials Budget Allocation Methods at San Diego County Library." Waznis, Betty. Co-published simultaneously in *The Acquisitions Librarian* (The Haworth Press, Inc.) No. 20, 1998, pp. 25-32; and: *Public Library Collection Development in the Information Age* (ed: Annabel K. Stephens) The Haworth Press, Inc., 1998, pp. 25-32. Single or multiple copies of this article are available for a fee from The Haworth Document Delivery Service [1-800-342-9678, 9:00 a.m. - 5:00 p.m. (EST). E-mail address: getinfo@haworthpressinc.com].

25

San Diego Public Library (with a large central research library and 33 neighborhood branches in the city of San Diego) and the cities of Carlsbad (one branch), Coronado, Chula Vista (two branches), Escondido (one branch), National City, and Oceanside (one branch).

The San Diego County Library employs 192 FTE staff, owns about 1.1 million volumes and circulates about 2.8 million items annually. The County Library runs 13 branch libraries in 11 incorporated cities, plus 18 branch libraries in communities in the unincorporated portion of the county. Two bookmobiles make weekly or monthly visits to the most remote parts of our service area.

The 1997-8 budget for San Diego County Library is $9.9 million. The materials budget is $820,000 plus $15,000 in anticipated revenue from book sales. In addition, many of our library branches are helped by Friends groups that add substantially to their neighborhood library book budget.

If you're not familiar with our part of the country, you may think of San Diego as just one big beach town. Our county is actually a large one, 4,261 square miles, with a lot of variety. You find many farms, ranches, a lot of rugged unpopulated mountainous terrain, big areas of desert, a long border with Mexico, small blue-collar and retirement communities as well as upper class education-minded areas and exclusive wealthy communities. San Diego County has one of the highest average housing costs in the US with one of the worst ratios of housing to income. It hosts a flourishing high-tech and biotech industry segment and each year welcomes a large number of immigrants, especially from the Pacific Rim, whose first language is not English.

County Library branches are found throughout this rich mix of small-town, rural, and suburban communities, from the horsey wealth of Rancho Santa Fe, to the tiny remote settlements of Jacumba and Potrero. We have crowded bustling branches in the urban setting of incorporated cities such as El Cajon, pleasant small-town sites in mountain retreats like Alpine and Julian, and neighborhood facilities in sophisticated beach towns like Encinitas, whose branch is perched on a cliff overlooking the Pacific.

The County Library service area is a "doughnut" around the City of San Diego (which runs its own municipal library system) without a natural center. The County Library has no "Main," no "Central," and no "downtown." We have no subject departments, no subject specialists, and no research sections. The Headquarters location functions only as an administrative and processing site which houses the Acquisitions and Cataloging Departments, the Interchange Division which provides sorting and delivery of books, a large Automation section, a graphic artist to make signs, flyers, and posters, the Outreach and Children's departments, and business, personnel, and administrative staff.

Our per capita book budget is 93 cents; that doesn't go far. The method used to divide the book budget is always of heated interest to many parties such as city councils, Friends groups, community and civic organizations, and taxpayers' associations. It's difficult to answer the question "What is my fair share?" so that all parties are satisfied. In an attempt to base our allocation decisions on the most complete, understandable, and objective factors, we collect and analyze quite a bit of information and consider a number of elements.

FACTORS USED FOR BUDGET ALLOCATION DECISIONS

Portion of Budget Allocated for Materials

What we start out with is the biggest determinant of what each branch will get. Our 31 far-flung facilities make us "house poor." Maintenance, rent, and upkeep are expenses not easily controlled. The library has decided to embark on an upgrade of its computer system and equipment. The book budget has failed to grow as the rest of the county budget has increased slowly but steadily over the past few years.

Core Service Levels

To get a handle on our unwieldy organization and to try to make more of the little we have, we find ourselves reorganizing constantly. We've relied on big geographic regional subdivisions, of which we've had five, three, and two at various times in the last ten years, overseen by six, four, or three supervising librarians. We've tried subdividing the geographic areas into "clusters," an idea which was short-lived. We've centralized and then decentralized children's service and service to underserved populations. In addition, we have developed branch category criteria, assigning all our branches to one of five service levels. The levels are determined by population, circulation, and square footage. We have used these levels to set minimum hours of service and staffing and number of volumes per capita. We found that the standards we developed are beyond our ability to fund, but it gives us something to aspire to and helps prevent allocation from being arbitrary.

Reference Needs

The closest large public reference center is the Central branch of San Diego Public Library, which is used by many of our patrons. Most California library systems subscribe to the practice of universal borrowing so that there is no fee for use by residents of other jurisdictions.

We have tried the "hub and spoke" system of reference service for many years. That is to say, our outlying rural branches have little or no reference resources and no reference staff. As you get closer to our large branches, reference service improves and increases.

Unfortunately, we are geographically challenged. In one of our regions, branches are clustered together and can take advantage of each others' resources fairly easily, but in other parts of our service areas, a customer might have to drive 20 miles or more to the nearest branch, which might not be bigger than his own. No matter how sensible it looks on paper, it is not practical to think that someone is going to drive an hour round trip to reach his designated "reference center."

This has left us to grapple with the need for information and reference service of all types in our smallest communities. Our medium-sized communities are growing; locations that only a short time ago were country hamlets are now booming commuter suburbs. We find that population distribution is "flattening": we have more towns and communities in the mid-population range instead of a few very large towns and a lot of tiny ones. We feel we have more towns and communities that need and can support a reference staff. Eight years ago only seven of our branches had a librarian on site; the others were expected to refer questions up. Today there are full-time reference librarians at ten sites, and half-time librarians at another five. So we have adjusted the money for reference to support an expanded reference function at these locations. We have decentralized reference and children's service into a large group of our branches in the second and third level. We purchased an online general, business, and health full-text service, a very practical step. We would buy more on-line sources if we had more OPACs in our branches to prevent "gridlock."

PUTTING THE BOOK BUDGET TOGETHER

We assemble the book budget annually. We reexamine each factor and assumption each year. There are three components to the book budget: base budgets, service-measurement allocations, and centralized expenditures.

Base Budgets

Each branch gets a "base," that is to say, a base level of funding depending on which service level group it belongs to. We put about one-third of our book budget into the "base" pool. Two groups of branches benefit most from this.

We have many tiny one-person branches in rural areas that would not get any money at all if they had to depend on their percentage of population, circulation, or tax revenue. So we assign each branch a base amount of money, a "floor" so that they have a minimum. The largest two branches have larger staffs and bear the burden of reference referrals, so they have a large "base" for that.

Service-Measurement Allocations

Population. The county's population has slowed down after a tremendous increase over the last two decades. A slight recession, coupled with the wind-down of defense-related industries that have long provided employment here, has equalized in and out migration during the past couple of years.

To assess population impact and make population adjustment, we consider the population of our branch service areas each year. Branch service areas were developed via an in-house study done in 1985. Traffic patterns, community planning districts, geographic and political boundaries, etc., were considered and service areas were defined. These may include an incorporated city only, an incorporated city with some surrounding unincorporated area, or wholly unincorporated areas.

To calculate population precisely, interim annual estimates are requested from the State Department of Revenue, which tracks births and deaths. Population figures can be obtained for incorporated cities. Census-tract estimates, further divided by community planning area boundaries, are supplied by the Department of Planning and Land Use, and are used for increased accuracy and refinement in the unincorporated areas.

Property Tax Revenue. Eighty percent of the County Library's funds come from a dedicated share of the property tax. County libraries are established under a section of the State Education Code to provide service to unincorporated areas and to any city that wishes to receive library service. Normally, service is not provided based on a contract. County library systems have traditionally collected tax money from the County Library service area as a whole, then dispersed it to fulfill service goals. This disbursement may have little relation to where the tax money originated. In many locations, individuals and local governments have become increasingly interested in determining if the amount of money that they pay in taxes each year is returned to them in library service. County library systems in our state are under a lot of pressure to "return to source" revenues of their member towns and communities. We have seen several instances in California where towns and communities were not satisfied that the county library system was giving them the library service they paid for, so they withdrew from the county system to form their own municipal or district library.

For these reasons we felt it was very important to assess property tax for each branch service area, whose boundaries don't coincide with anything else. Property tax is reported by our Department of Revenue as one lump sum for the unincorporated area. To correctly derive tax revenue for our branch service areas, we completed a nine-month project of assigning each tax rate area (which could be as small as a part of a street or a block) to a branch service area, then added all the tax rate areas together for each branch service area. Of course, the tax rate areas do not perfectly coincide with our branch service area boundaries. Nonetheless, the estimate is a very good one, far better than we could get using any other technique. Although time consuming and tedious, this has been very worthwhile. Many locations which suspected that they might be "donors" have turned out to receive more in service than they pay in taxes.

Circulation. Circulation is one of the factors we consider, but only one. When circulation is the only or the most weighted factor used in allocation, the rich get richer and the poor get poorer. We evaluate and use circulation statistics, trying to reward those locations that do a good job of selecting and displaying their materials. We also try to remember that you can't circulate what you can't afford to buy and that many of our locations are very short on space and are forced to limit the choices their patrons have because of lack of shelf space.

Centralized Expenditures

This includes videos, bestsellers, any special projects we want to fund, children's, literacy, outreach, and other systemwide expenditures.

Videos are wholly funded by a fifty cent fee charged to ensure their return and condition. This raises about $38,000 annually.

Bestsellers are ordered centrally. We reserve about $30,000 for this aspect of the collection.

The Children's Department is allocated some money for special projects. (This is apart from and in addition to the money allocated to each branch, a substantial part of which is spent for children at every location.) Children's Department staff have planned Homework Helper Centers, added to "Grandparents and Books" story time collections, and have used these funds for other one-time and rotating resources.

Outreach/Non-English speaking populations. In response to the increase of non-English speakers in our county, the budget for non-English language materials was increased to about ten percent of the branch book budget. In the past couple of years we have experimented with moving beyond only using census demographic information (which gets more dated the further in time you move away from the Census) and thereby providing increased money for the "known" communities of high Spanish-speaking population. We are now trying a straight percentage allocation so that each branch gets its overall percentage, not a budget depending on its demographic profile. All of our towns and communities have residents whose first language is not English. There are many Spanish speakers, but also speakers of Chinese, Vietnamese, Arabic, and other non-European languages. Our local government statistical bureau provides good yearly estimates of population changes, but not to the level of ethnic composition. We were conscious that the census figures recording ethnic make-up were probably out of date due to the very high level of immigration into our county in the past decade. We felt that we needed to see beyond the traditional patterns of population of 8 or 10 years ago and try "seeding" some of our other communities with additional funds in hopes of bringing in more readers. The Outreach Department disburses most of these funds directly to branches. The money can be spent on non-English language magazines which are selected once a year and also on an annual series of three non-English selection lists (one adult, one juvenile, and one audio-visual). Branch staff can also visit bookstores that cater to non-English speaking populations and buy retail if the venue is approved in advance.

In addition, the Outreach Department pays for and organizes "Heritage Month Celebrations" to encourage interest in our non-English collections. For instance, if branches sign up for Hispanic Heritage Month or Asian-Pacific Heritage Month, they promise to do a program a week and in exchange get about $300 worth of books and materials.

Literacy. This area is heavily supported by the State Library, which has provided funding through the federally-sponsored Library Services and Construction Act. Part of these funds is spent to support literacy instruction and services at the Adult Literacy Services office. The remainder of the funds is allocated to the branches using the same methodology as for the branch budget as a whole and is spent on circulating literacy materials used by tutors at branch locations and by the general public.

Electronic online resources. The purchase of a full-text magazine database has been hugely popular and successful. In our widespread system it is the most practical way to provide information to our rural locations. Even the branches not staffed by librarians have found it very usable since the public can use it easily. We were fortunate to find an alternate funding source for this.

We are exploring a better method of selecting and paying for on-line and other system-wide services. We have maintained a highly decentralized system of resource selection because it suits our conglomeration of political and regional communities. It has made a lot of users, Friends groups, local politicians and tax-payers happy. But it makes it difficult to take money "off the top" for big projects that benefit everyone. In a system where no one, even the most wealthy, has enough money and everyone intends to hold on to their "fair share," a big-dollar cooperative selection project takes a lot of preparation.

FINAL CALCULATION

To prepare the final budget spreadsheet we take the allocations for system-wide services "off the top." We assign and subtract the branch base amounts. Then we allocate the remainder based on each branch's percentage of population, circulation, or tax revenue.

Our book budget is fully allocated. That is to say, the system-wide portions are allocated to each branch based either on anticipated projects where exact dollar amounts for each location are known in advance, or via a percentage allocation where, for instance, each branch gets bestsellers based on its overall percentage of the book budget. So our final budget picture shows all dollars in the branch budgets and nothing costed to Central divisions.

CONCLUSION

Many California county libraries currently find themselves in difficult financial and political situations, but we always have hope for a better year ahead. San Diego County Library has managed to keep its very diverse communities functioning as a whole. We have done so through diligent attention to precise cost accounting for all jurisdictions and functions, and through willingness to share detailed financial information with our constituent cities and Friends groups. When they see the sorry picture our spreadsheets paint, they believe us when we say that they are getting the best deal we can possibly give them, that there is no hidden money or bloated bureaucracy, and that we welcome them as full partners in our neverending effort to improve library service for our customers.

"But We've Always Done It This Way!" Centralized Selection Five Years Later

Catherine Gibson

SUMMARY. Even though many librarians want to think that their communities are unique and that they alone can order effectively for their patrons, mounting research indicates that readers in the United States are influenced more by the media and what is published and promoted, than by local factors, when they select items to read. Centralized selection can be a successful way to allocate additional staff time to direct public service without sacrificing the utility of local collections. *[Article copies available for a fee from The Haworth Document Delivery Service: 1-800-342-9678. E-mail address: getinfo@haworthpressinc.com]*

The Indianapolis-Marion County Public Library's reasons for instituting centralized selection probably do not differ significantly from other medium to large public library systems that have adopted similar measures. "The way we've always done things" just didn't stand up to the pressures of increased demands for public service, rising costs, political realities and finite resources. In order to protect the percent of the total budget that would be allocated to materials and on-line resources and to redirect additional staff time to direct public service, we determined that

Catherine Gibson is Manager of Adult Services at the Indianapolis-Marion County Public Library, P.O. Box 211, Indianapolis, IN 46206-0211. Her undergraduate degree and MLS are from Indiana University.

The author wishes to thank previous and current Adult Collection Development Librarians Laura Bramble, Elaine Potter and Theresa Butler, for their assistance.

[Haworth co-indexing entry note]: " 'But We've Always Done It This Way!' Centralized Selection Five Years Later." Gibson, Catherine. Co-published simultaneously in *The Acquisitions Librarian* (The Haworth Press, Inc.) No. 20, 1998, pp. 33-40; and: *Public Library Collection Development in the Information Age* (ed: Annabel K. Stephens) The Haworth Press, Inc., 1998, pp. 33-40. Single or multiple copies of this article are available for a fee from The Haworth Document Delivery Service [1-800-342-9678, 9:00 a.m. - 5:00 p.m. (EST). E-mail address: getinfo@haworthpressinc.com].

reducing the number of staff involved in the selection of materials was our best course.

Was this a popular decision? Of course not! In preparation for the change the Director, Ray Gnat, commissioned a team from the School of Public Administration at Indiana University-Purdue University at Indianapolis to analyze the circulation data of all our agencies. The resulting data showed that there were only two areas, westerns and travel books, that showed slight statistically significant differences in circulation patterns from branch to branch, from regional branches to storefronts, from center city agencies to those in the suburbs. Travel books circulated better in the affluent suburban branches, and the branch that was located in the one area of the county that still had working farms had a slight edge in western circulation. The resulting report, "Similarities in Circulation Patterns Among Public Library Branches Serving Diverse Populations"[1] concluded that, based on the Indianapolis data, "persons who checked out and read books tended to read very similar types of materials without regard to the characteristics of the populations served by the branches. Furthermore, circulation patterns in the branches were only weakly related to the social and economic characteristics of the populations served by the branches." The study suggests that the ability to read and to be comfortable with that activity is a stronger determining factor in what types of materials will be read than age, sex, race, and education or income levels.

Until the publication of Hazel M. Davis and Ellen Altman's "The Relationship Between Community Lifestyles and Circulation Patterns in Public Libraries"[2] in the January/February 1997 issue of *Public Libraries,* which reported similar findings using a much larger sample (eight million circulation records from ten different communities), I had been cautious about even suggesting that libraries in other metropolitan areas would have similar results if they replicated this study. I have heard from too many librarians across the country who were certain that their communities were unique, to suggest that these studies are conclusive; however, the Davis/Altman article suggests a few follow-up studies. One is particularly worthy of study before we think that we have any "scientific" evidence that people want to read the same things. Davis and Altman wonder if collections are similar because many libraries use the same selection tools (*Booklist* and *Library Journal*). An equally strong possibility is that patrons in all U.S. libraries are influenced by the same media, in this case *People,* Oprah, "Fresh Air," etc., and that we are more of a global village than we like to admit from our cloaks of "we are the only ones who can select for our patrons."

In an article on the book publishing industry, Ken Auletta quotes from Michael Naumann of Henry Holt:

> That's the big story. This deeply pluralistic, multifaceted, multieth-nic, multiregionally divided hierarchic country has such orderly tastes. Everybody seems to have the same taste.[3]

And even if that weren't true, Charlie Robinson points out the obvious in a recent editorial in the *Library Administrator's Digest* that all libraries are selecting from what the publishers decide to publish and then to keep in print.[4] Just because your library might need new tree identification books to help with that perennial school assignment doesn't mean that publishers are rushing to issue titles with lots of pictures and a fifth grade reading level.

We made the decision to move forward with centralized selection based on the information about how our patrons were using our existing collections. I wrote a position paper for the Library Board outlining our rationale for centralized selection. I included a time table and list of related activities. The system would be phased in over an eighteen-month period. Ironically one of the related activities I proposed was a massive Central/branch staff exchange to promote a better understanding of the differing communities and public uses of the collections. The branch and Central adult services librarians and managers would switch places for two months. The commotion this created made the move to centralized selection pale in terms of staff controversy!

Before centralized selection, each librarian at Central was responsible for a discrete area of the collection based on Dewey classification. The first or "Central copy" of each new item was cataloged and sent to an area called the New Book Room where it stayed for one week. During that week each branch sent one to four librarians to this area to select the items they wanted for their agencies. These first copies were unavailable to the public for at least two weeks for this process, and then Acquisitions had to submit a second order for the branch copies. Even before full centralized selection we were placing all fiction orders from early reviews and not the first copies so they could be processed as a group. When lease collections were phased out the Manager of Adult Services started placing the system orders for multiple copies of titles on the prepub-potential-best seller lists sent by jobbers.

Thinking back to that way of selection two things are striking. One is the large amount of staff time involved in having librarians from twenty-one branches driving to the Central Library and spending anywhere from one to four hours looking at "new" books; the other, the delay in getting new materials out to the public. If it were suggested that we return to that form of selection the outcry from branch managers for more staff would be immediate.

As we moved to implement total centralized selection, a new position, Collection Development Librarian, was added; and this person assumed responsibility for ordering titles from prepub alert sheets, *Booklist* and *Publisher's Weekly* for Central and the branches. The Central librarians used the other selection sources to initiate orders for all the other materials to flesh out their respective areas. Now the Collection Development Librarian goes over these Central orders and adds the branch copies. All orders have to arrive at and leave her desk within forty-eight hours. During vacations or illness someone else has to make sure that time frame is maintained. Decisions have to be made rapidly and continuously. Very few titles can be put aside to ponder. We try to get the right number of copies on the first order, but we use the weekly "purchase alert" list which indicates titles with more than two holds per copy to generate orders for additional copies.

We are constantly tinkering with the system trying to streamline procedures. We are currently stymied in our efforts to get to a paperless and electronic ordering system, but we are confident that we can resolve those problems in the next eighteen months. Centralized selection has saved a significant amount of public service time in the branches, but we are still examining ways to get similar time savings at Central. The staff deserves the credit for the successes of this system of selection. It would have been easy for branch staff to bad-mouth the process to patrons any time a desired item was not on the shelf; however, I have had only one public complaint that had even a tinge of that sentiment. That is remarkable considering that we have forms at the service desks that invite the public to jot a note to the Director if they have concerns.

Centralized selection is five years old in Indianapolis. The circulation figures continue to climb. Possibly because we encourage patron input with Request for Purchase and Reserve postals that are answered promptly and a web version of the same form that can be responded to within hours, we do not get more than a handful of complaints about what is not in the collections. Because of various changes in the way we keep track of statistics we don't have precise circulation figures by agency. We know the number of items that are checked out by agency, but since we instituted phone and on-line web renewal we only have aggregate figures for renewals. Certainly no staff members in any library building are complaining that business is slacking off.

KNOWLEDGE OF THE COMMUNITY

Putting the library users aside for the moment, the rather standard objection to centralized selection within the profession is that a librarian working out of a central office cannot know the needs of a given community so well as the librarian who is working in that community every day. To respond to this objection I fall back on some of my personal experiences in that sacred area, "knowledge of the community." The reader will have to determine if these observations are anecdotal or have kernels of validity. When I was the manager of a medium-sized branch, the staff got into a discussion about our "average" patron. Staff agreed that our most frequent users were Anglo women who were at or approaching retirement age. We decided to test our assumptions in a manner that wouldn't pass any doctoral review panel, but might give us a little direction. We did simple age, sex, and race tallies on the people we saw enter the branch. Within a week we had lost all faith in our powers of observation. The group we thought was typical made up a small percentage of our users; however, the group that we thought it would take a massive free stereo giveaway program to lure through our doors, the young adults, were our largest group of users. It didn't take us long to realize that the mature women were the patrons who talked to us the most and for whom no doubt we were selecting. The younger users may or may not have been getting what they wanted but they were not interacting voluntarily with us one way or the other.

I frequently use the example of the perfectly conscientious librarian who told me that she had one gay patron who used her library. That perception had to color the selections she was making for her branch. (Perhaps she misunderstood the statistic and thought it was one in every thousand! Even then she was statistically assured of at least thirty-four in her service area.) Even in an area that would seem more obvious, it was only after centralized selection that we began to dramatically expand our African-American materials in the collections of the suburban branches where many of the African-American population live. My contention is simply this: we make too much and too little of our knowledge of our communities. Research on library use patterns has told us many times in the past that librarians do not have direct contact with well over half of the people who use our facilities. We draw our conclusions from the people who seek us out or whom we approach.

Despite those caveats we still want and expect the Collection Development Librarian to know as much about each branch community as possible while maintaining an open mind and not making limiting assumptions about a particular community. Maintaining centralized selection has been both easier and harder than imagined. We knew from the beginning that communication among the Collection Development Librarian, the branch personnel and the Central subject selectors would spell success or failure. The first year the Collection Development Librarian spent the better part of a week at each branch agency talking with staff and working the public service desks trying to soak up as much of a feel for each agency's clientele and recurring requests as possible. Unlike some centralized selection plans we did not allocate a certain dollar amount to each agency for replacement orders. Agencies could send in as many or as few replacement titles as they wished or needed. Some of the small and medium-sized agencies sent in few replacement titles but instead relied on new titles in specific subject areas of the collection that they indicated in their profiles were in steady demand. In addition to the visits to the branches by the Collection Development Librarian, there is a computerized file of subject needs maintained for each agency. Branch personnel are encouraged to send updates to their profiles and review their file twice a year to see if particular subject area needs have been fulfilled or are still active. This simple database, with subject headings that would make Sears and LC wince, is functional.

In subsequent years the Collection Development Librarian has made shorter visits to all the branch agencies. Annually the Manager of Adult Services, the Collection Development Librarian and the head Adult Services librarian from each agency sit down and outline collection development goals for the coming year.

Just because the majority of the collection is ordered centrally does not mean that the local staffs can ignore the collection. Once a title is ordered staff in the local agency can determine if it was ordered for their agency and in what quantity. If they feel that their agency needs the title but it was not ordered for them, they can initiate an order immediately. They know that very few titles reviewed in *Booklist* or *Publisher's Weekly* will be skipped for the system. They are encouraged to read the reviews, examine the books when they arrive, initiate replacement orders, notify the Collection Development Librarian of new homework assignments and areas of the collections that need new or additional materials, and finally to maintain continuous weeding. They are responsible for determining which titles they want on standing order and which periodicals to add or drop. Because the majority of our branch buildings were erected before the proliferation of formats and the electronic revolution, all agencies are struggling to find space for more terminals, better display space for books, audiocassettes, compact disks and videocassettes, and to determine the amount of space to be allocated to each format. In reality any time that was saved by turning to centralized selection has been eaten up by staff shifting and rearranging to accommodate the expanding non-print formats, learning to use the new electronic resources and to navigate the Internet while coping with expanding business.

COLLECTION DIVERSITY

One of the goals of centralized selection was to increase the diversity in the branch collections and to avoid as much personal and cost bias as possible.[5] Gender and education biases were problems whether we wanted to admit them or not. With only one male adult services administrator in the branches at the time centralized selection was instituted and a staff full of liberal arts majors, the collections did have decidedly female and arts/ humanities focuses. The preponderance of the non-fiction collections were strong in history and literature even though every circulation analysis indicated that these were not the strongest circulating areas. The sciences and computer sections were weak, not just because these were areas outside of the comfortable knowledge bases of the branch selectors, but also because of cost. It was difficult for the branch selector to spend $75 for a basic chemistry or physics text when funds were limited. The hard-to-fight "but we are going to lose the book anyway" syndrome also had chilling effects in the true crime, sexuality, and occult areas. Ironically there were some "feminine" areas of the collection that were also weak. We lacked any depth in basic sewing, and the home decorating areas had a variety of titles but not enough multiple copies to insure that something was on the shelf at any given time. On the other hand, even librarians who didn't cook seemed to understand instinctively that many people did!

We learn about self censoring in library school and all try to avoid it, but if a librarian is opposed to guns it is hard to acknowledge that one book on guns or hunting does not an adequate collection make. Obviously selection centralized in one Collection Development Librarian could exacerbate those problems. It would be safe to say that even though there is little grumbling now about centralized selection, other librarians are watching what is ordered and haven't been shy about pointing out areas with too much or too little emphasis. Again the requests from the public play an important role. So far we have been lucky enough to maintain a ratio of one copy for each two holds and each week a list of titles that fall outside that formula is generated by the automation system. That list is checked promptly and "beef-up" replacement orders treated as rush items in Technical Services. This list gives me the opportunity to determine if there are any patterns in titles that we are ordering "short." I annotate the list and give portions of it back to the Collection Development Librarian.

Through some unusual quirks we have had three different individuals serving as Collection Development Librarian in the first five years. All have done outstanding jobs in the position, but none stayed long enough to get in any sort of a rut.

THE FUTURE

There is no doubt that centralized selection is here to stay, but the process will adapt to take advantage of changes in technology. We have organized a redesign team within the library system that is taking a look at how we can create a paperless selection and acquisitions system and fully implement electronic ordering. Jobbers and automation systems vendors are making new inroads in electronic convenience for librarians, and the future will see stronger cooperation between jobbers, automation systems and acquisitions librarians.

REFERENCES

1. John R. Ottensmann, Raymond E. Gnat, and Michael E. Gleeson, "Similarities in Circulation Patterns Among Public Library Branches Serving Diverse Populations," *Library Quarterly* 65 (Jan. 1995): 89-118.

2. Hazel M. Davis and Ellen Altman, "The Relationship Between Community Lifestyles and Circulation Patterns in Public Libraries," *Public Libraries* 36 (January/February 1997): 40-45.

3. Ken Auletta, "The Impossible Business," *The New Yorker* 73 (October 6, 1997): 50-63.

4. "From the Editor's Desk," *Library Administrator's Digest* 32 (September, 1997): 53.

5. Catherine Gibson, "How We Spent $2.7 Million–With the Help of Centralized Selection," *Library Journal* 120 (September 1, 1995): 128-130.

Five Levels
of Vendor-Assisted
Collection Development

Lauren K. Lee

SUMMARY. Vendor assistance in public library collection development is not an all-or-nothing proposition. There are a wide range of services available which should be chosen according to library needs and comfort factors. This article discusses the information and evaluation involved in selection plus the communication required in a cooperative selection process. Five levels of vendor assistance are also delineated. *[Article copies available for a fee from The Haworth Document Delivery Service: 1-800-342-9678. E-mail address: getinfo@haworthpressinc.com]*

Vendor assistance in public library collection development can assume a wide variety of forms ranging from published catalogs or online databases that facilitate selection to completely outsourced title selection and distribution. This article will discuss the three requirements for such cooperative processes and will detail the levels of selection assistance as currently defined by the Brodart Company.

In selecting materials for public libraries, two processes are required—information gathering and the evaluation of that information, with purchase decisions as the ultimate goal. When a vendor becomes involved in the process as well, a third intermediary step is required—communication.

Lauren K. Lee is Manager of Collection Development Services at the Brodart Company, 500 Arch Street, Williamsport, PA 17705.

[Haworth co-indexing entry note]: "Five Levels of Vendor-Assisted Collection Development." Lee, Lauren K. Co-published simultaneously in *The Acquisitions Librarian* (The Haworth Press, Inc.) No. 20, 1998, pp. 41-51; and: *Public Library Collection Development in the Information Age* (ed: Annabel K. Stephens) The Haworth Press, Inc., 1998, pp. 41-51. Single or multiple copies of this article are available for a fee from The Haworth Document Delivery Service [1-800-342-9678, 9:00 a.m. - 5:00 p.m. (EST). E-mail address: getinfo@haworthpressinc.com].

INFORMATION

Obviously you can't make selection decisions until you have a title or group of titles from which to select and a framework for decision-making. This information is then of two types: local information and global information. The local information provides the background for decision-making and includes such things as collection size and content, analysis of the community served, circulation patterns, current budget situation, selection policy and collection development goals. This local information exists first and foremost in the minds and memories of local selectors, ideally backed up by written documents.

The second type of information, which for this purpose I will call global, concerns the materials being considered for purchase. What exactly is available? How much does it cost? Where can it be obtained? How good is it? How popular will it be? The bare minimum for a new title would be the fact that an item exists (or will within a few months), the author, the publisher, the price, the all-important ISBN, the binding and/or physical format. For an older title, we must add the current availability status. It existed once, but is it still available?

The next layer of information on a title would be more descriptive. Is this title part of a series? How is it classified? What subject headings or terms best describe it? How many pages does it have? Is it illustrated? Is its cover attractive? What does the table of contents promise? How does its publisher describe it?

The third layer gives an indication of the item's quality. Does it deliver what it promised? How good is it? Who has reviewed it? What have they said? Is it recommended for public library collections? Has it won any awards or been cited in any bibliographies? This can be as simple as links to sources of data (e.g., review or bibliography citations) or the actual information can be drawn together in some manner. In the past, this "drawing together" might happen in file boxes of three-by-five cards or on photocopied sheets of paper. At best, the data would be brought together in a local database, perhaps along with comments of local selectors.

This qualitative information boils down to what others have said in their evaluation process of the title. This evaluation might be from either a paid professional or a volunteer reviewer. Or it could be from a vendor predicting popularity and patron demand by analyzing past sales by the author, information from the publisher, or plans for advertising and promotion. For an older title it would include awards it has won, bibliographies that have cited it, and perhaps how well it has sold. This global information begins with publishers and must be transmitted to vendors, review journals, and database proprietors (certainly the Books in Print database and, now just as importantly, vendor databases and cataloging utilities). Along the way, the mass media picks up some of the information, as do public library patrons. Local selectors can find this information in review journals, publisher catalogs, vendor catalogs, advertisements, mass media, or the line of patrons at the desk.

In this information age, it is the method of transmission of global information that has changed the most. We're not just passing information on paper (though there's still plenty of that happening). Vendors are now offering databases for libraries to search, sending records electronically, and interfacing with integrated library systems.

COMMUNICATION

When vendors assist in transmitting this global information to the local level, effective communication is required. Therefore, the vendor must be able to articulate to the professional community the services that are available; to whom they are available; the cost, if any; and how those services can be used. This, too, can happen in a number of ways–advertisements, literature, presentations, one-to-one communication, or word of mouth. Unfortunately, vendor services usually play only a small part in library school curricula.

One-way communication is not enough, however, when vendor assistance moves from the generic catalog or database to the provision of a custom service or product. Information must then also flow from librarian to vendor describing what is needed. In requesting a list of titles on a given subject area, the librarian must be able to describe the subject in a way that the vendor can then translate to their own system, perhaps Dewey classification ranges. Or, if moving to complete outsourcing, extensive communication is needed. Each public library has its own selection policies, procedures, and collection goals. The more thoroughly these can be described to the vendor, the more successful the project can be. The vendor staff needs to understand the selection process that has been in place, who has been responsible for selection, what tools have been used, and what selection criteria are most important.

Finally, the communication returns from vendor to librarian in a body of titles that meet the need. This can be not only the titles themselves but also a description of how they were compiled.

EVALUATION

Now that information about a group of titles has been gathered, it is time for evaluation of those titles against the local selection criteria. This is where the level of vendor involvement may range from the mere provision of availability information to actual selection and distribution. At the most generic level, this involves the publication of catalogs or compact discs or the posting of databases. The vendor is offering a group of titles to an audience that has shared interests and needs. It is expected that all evaluation and filtering of titles will be done by the local staff. In the case of compact discs and databases, title by title searching will also be done by local staff.

This generic model is, indeed, the most common model due to its very simplicity. It is the purpose of this article, however, to explore the more intricate model of customized collection development on the part of the vendor. Up to this point, I have been speaking of "the vendor" in general and universally applicable terms. As I proceed to discuss the various levels of customized assistance, I will rely primarily on those services offered by the Brodart Company Books Division, with which I am most familiar.

BRODART'S FIVE LEVELS OF ASSISTANCE

Brodart's collection development services began in the mid-1980s with several large opening day collection projects. Indeed, Brodart's original selection list programming was designed with retrospective collection development in mind. It combined availability information with evaluative information, the latter coming primarily from published bibliographies and awards lists. Over the years, the original programming was enhanced, as was the number and variety of bibliographies and other sources used to create lists. In 1993, a service designed for new title selection in public libraries was introduced–Title Information Preview Service (TIPS). It was the first vendor service to provide full text reviews of recent publications from multiple journals on custom selection lists. Janet Majilton, Collection Development Officer for the Memphis-Shelby County Public Library and Information Center, has said that the physical format of the TIPS lists makes it easier to efficiently share this information among selectors than the journal issues themselves.

Over the years the two types of selection lists, retrospective lists now called Collection Builders, and TIPS lists, have been used by hundreds of public, school and academic libraries with widely different needs. After not only observing, but also actively participating in the provision of these services, staff members Linda Homa, Marc Stiger, and I devised a system of describing the varying levels of vendor participation in the evaluation of titles. The five levels are described below, showing a gradual shift from a model with little or no vendor evaluation to a model that leaves all evaluation and distribution of titles to the vendor.

Level One, or the Automated Level

Library describes their needs; vendor produces custom list from its database using the library's specifications. On the vendor side, this is primarily an automated process. The professional involvement is on the front end with initial communication followed by design of lists. Once generated, these lists receive little or no review by the vendor. The local library staff is evaluating titles from an unedited list. In the arena of new titles, most TIPS lists fit this level.

For example, the Las Vegas-Clark County Library District has a number of TIPS profiles for their adult collection. There are separate adult fiction and nonfiction profiles for the urban libraries and separate adult fiction and nonfiction profiles for their extension libraries. They also have specialized profiles for reference, health sciences, and African-American interest. The initial design may be complicated, but the automated system takes over as soon as the specifications are set.

Many automatic orders are also at this level; for example, the library might provide a list of authors whose new hardcover fiction works would be automatically ordered at a set quantity. The Free Library of Philadelphia began using TIPS lists in the fall of 1993 for adult titles that were reviewed that they were not receiving through their own gathering plans. Less than a year later, they asked Brodart to supply first copies of titles from those same publishers in addition to providing their TIPS selection list.

With retrospective needs, many Collection Builders would be at this level. A library might ask for a list of titles from Phase One of *The Elementary School Library Collection,* along with *Children's Catalog* (our two most frequently-requested juvenile sources). Another might ask for the most popular computer books or Dewey 500's. With these lists there is no need for the vendor to evaluate the results.

Level Two, or the Edited Level

At Level Two, the vendor involvement picks up a bit. The needs are described and the custom list is produced as above, but the vendor performs some editing on the list. A staff member from the vendor now gets involved not only in the front end list design but also in the back end evaluation of the success of the list. At Level Two, however, this involvement is still minimal. Someone might eliminate out-of-scope titles or multiple binds of the same title (e.g., retain the hardcover but eliminate the paperback when both are available). In this model, the library profiles the need, the vendor's computer produces the list, the vendor reviews it and makes minor modifications, and the local librarian evaluates the titles and makes the final decisions. Or, the order might not be truly automatic at all. The vendor's computer generates the order, but the vendor faxes the order-to-be to the library for approval. Once approved or modified, the order is actually placed.

Why is more vendor involvement sometimes needed? Perhaps the filtering is not something that can be completely controlled by automated parameters. The vendor staff can assist the librarian by eliminating titles that are obviously not appropriate. It might be done at the request of a library that lacks qualified staff or that wants to redeploy professional talent.

For new titles, there are some "automatic" orders that are reviewed and modified by the vendor. The Los Angeles Public Library has an automatic order that they use for review copies of adult nonfiction. It is based on a list of publishers. We manually review the titles in order to decide which edition to supply in the case of simultaneous publication of hardcover and paperback. With automatic orders by author, we watch out for those "three books in one" editions that retail may love but librarians hate. An example of Level Two editing of retrospective materials is choosing the "best" editions of classics, or at least eliminating the oddball editions.

Level Three, or the Preselected Level

At Level Three the vendor actually begins to "preselect" titles from custom lists it generates and from other sources. Our professional involvement increases significantly at this level. Not only do we review the initial lists we generate but we also search out specific titles or types of titles. We check for balance and comprehensiveness of the list. At Level Three, the evaluation of titles is fairly evenly divided between vendor and local staff. The library, as always, describes their need. The vendor then creates a list in a two-step rather than a one-step process. The library still decides what to buy, but from a very polished list.

For new titles, Brodart's best example is the McNaughton Book Service, used by libraries for over fifty years. Though thought of primarily as an adult hardcover bestseller service, McNaughton also offers hardcover plans for young adults and children, as well as a paperback plan. McNaughton itself is a book leasing and subscription program but the titles selected for inclusion in the program are also offered to Brodart customers for purchase.

The titles are selected by committees charged with identifying and selecting the titles that libraries can't afford to miss. The adult committee meets twice a month and reviews the titles due to be published four months later. This list is finalized and distributed to customers at the "three month prepub" point. The current committee has over one hundred years of combined experience in choosing McNaughton titles.

Level Three for retrospective titles could be replacement lists for specific subjects or entire opening day collections. Once again this could be a parameter that could not be translated to an automated system. Some of my favorites are instructions to exclude obscure poetry books and personal narratives of completely unknown people. Another example of subjective decisions would be to include titles with two or more positive reviews. What constitutes a positive review? How positive must the review be?

Another example of Level Three would be the use and manipulation of library holdings information in the creation of selection lists. Here, the vendor involvement is not so much in evaluating titles but in processing holdings files in a way that can be useful to the library in the evaluation process. Sometimes a library might want to buy only picture books that were already in their collection. Others might want to compare their holdings to a bibliography with plans to purchase titles they do not already own. This use of holdings information can be as simple as copying an entire database of bibliographic records, or as complex as splitting that database into collection codes or multiple locations.

Level Four, or the Selected Level

Level Four approaches full transfer of title evaluation from library to vendor. At this level, we not only preselect titles, we actually select them and then order them for a single location (Level Five covers multiple locations). The library profiles the needs; the vendor selects; the library receives, first, a report of what has been ordered on their behalf, and, second, the books themselves. This is different from the automatic orders above, in that a librarian on the vendor's staff is evaluating titles against the library's needs and selecting them accordingly. This calls for a complete transfer of the local information–selection policy, project budget, collection goals and proportions, as well as areas of emphasis, need for multiple copies, and binding preferences.

Level Four is most common with opening day collections. The Chicago Public Library has contracted with Brodart since 1989 for shelf-ready collections for their new branches. They receive a copy of the selections before the orders are entered, so that quantities can be changed or a few title substitutions made.

Level Five, or the Selected and Distributed Level

At Level Four the vendor has made the final selection decisions. Now, at Level Five, those title decisions are reevaluated with system distribution in mind. First the appropriate titles are selected; then quantities are set and specific locations are assigned. The local information required becomes more complicated depending on the number of locations involved, the range of budget amounts, and the homogeneity or heterogeneity of all the collections. This level obviously requires the most intensive professional involvement of them all. Not only is title, author, publisher, and general selection expertise required of the vendor, but also administrative, organizational and communication skills. Level Five requires tracking volumes by category and funds by location.

Level Five is still relatively rare. Even though Brodart was not involved, the reengineering project undertaken in 1996 by the Hawaii State Public Library System could be described as 100% Level Five vendor selection.

Brodart's current example of Level Five selection is the Fort Worth Public Library's juvenile collection. Since January 1994 we have selected the new juvenile titles for their main library and eleven branches. They retain a percentage of their budgets for replacement orders and some discretionary purchasing of new juvenile titles. They do not outsource their adult selection. Brodart's selector, Linda Homa, uses layered TIPS profiles to identify titles. She is given guidelines of which authors and illustrators and series to purchase regardless of review. The remaining selections are based on her comparison of reviews from several journals.

Of course, good communication is required of the library staff as well. They must define the policies and preferences that guide the library but also the differences among each of the branches. The "local" selector is no longer physically local, but must understand the communities to be served, the roles of the libraries, the current collections, the areas of high and low demand, and the budgets by collection category and media. In order to be effective these profiles must be reviewed, revised, and updated annually or whenever circumstances change significantly. Catherine Dixon, Assistant Director at Fort Worth, stresses that the library staff and vendor staff must consider themselves partners in a cooperative process.

Combination Approaches

Libraries using vendor services can choose a different level for each part of the collection. For example, new adult bestsellers could be Level

One (automated) automatic orders, while the remainder of reviewed titles could be handled through a Level One TIPS profile. Juvenile titles could be locally selected from preselected, Level Three vendor lists.

To give some examples from Brodart's current customers, the Memphis-Shelby County Public Library and Information Center requests subject replacement lists, both adult and juvenile, that tend to be Levels Two (edited) and Three (preselected). They also receive automatic, Level One TIPS lists that are compiled from various journals.

The Los Angeles Public Library's automatic order for review copies of adult nonfiction is Level Two (edited). We choose between hardcovers and paperbacks of the same title based on a price formula and cancel some unwanted items like daily devotionals and books intended for the gift market. They use these copies to decide on multiples for the Central Library and to identify titles for possible branch purchases. Then the Central Library receives TIPS lists for non-bestseller fiction and for a wide range of nonfiction (Level One), excluding the titles that have been ordered for them. These books are also considered for the system when they arrive.

The Detroit Public Library has also begun to use an automatic order for first copies of adult materials. However, their profile uses journals to identify titles rather than publishers. This automatic order is also Level Two (edited) because we choose between hardcover and paperback editions of the same title using a price formula. Robert Chapman has described the process which led them to this approach in an article in *Against the Grain,* September 1997.

Several libraries have more interactive models. The Library Network in suburban Detroit (TLN) has had three (3) Level One (automated) TIPS profiles since 1993–one for children's materials, one for young adult, and one for adult nonfiction. The three profiles use a combination of titles from various journals, publishers, and series. At the beginning of each monthly cycle they receive draft lists both on paper and electronically. The staff at TLN headquarters edits those lists, deleting such things as obscure poetry and adding some local titles and new serial editions. They send that information back to Brodart electronically, where final lists are produced. At the same time, an automatic order is placed for all items. These first copies are put on display and member libraries have the option of reviewing the books and/or selecting from their copies of the final lists.

The Sno-Isle Regional Library System (Marysville, Washington) receives Level One TIPS lists for both adult and juvenile materials. They also request Collection Builder lists on a regular basis. In 1997, their lists were Level Three due to extensive manipulation of holdings information and thorough review of the lists by the vendor before they were sent.

ELECTRONIC COMMUNICATION

Up to this point I have discussed the content of the lists more than the physical format of them. Many of the scenarios described above rely on computer-generated, printed lists. Electronic transmission of these lists is, however, becoming much more common, particularly for new title lists (they tend to be smaller and more manageable electronically than retrospective lists). The Library Network's editing process, as described above, is made possible by sharing and swapping electronic files between the library and the vendor. Brodart's PC Rose Plus software is the mechanism used. The Harris County Library (Houston, Texas) also uses a similar process. The editing is done through PC Rose, but the final files are provided in a MARC-like format for loading into their Dynix system.

The Alameda County Library pioneered loading MARC-formatted selection records in late 1994. They wrote script files that made it easy to import TIPS records into their Innovative Interfaces system and to make selection lists available online to all their libraries. The branches can do their title evaluation from the printed lists or directly online. Their orders, however, must be placed online and are, therefore, quite easily consolidated and transmitted by their Acquisitions department.

CONCLUSION

Levels One (automated) and Two (edited) are certainly the most common. The cost for these services can range from gratis to subscription fees for the full text reviews that are part of TIPS lists. These two levels delegate title identification to the vendor, making use of the vendor's database and automated systems. The library staff is still actively involved in evaluating titles and making decisions. Level Three (preselected) involves sharing title evaluation between the library and the vendor. More professional involvement is required on the part of the vendor, therefore, there are usually some costs associated with these services. Levels Four (selected) and Five (selected and distributed) are the most challenging for the vendor (and perhaps the library as well!). It is certainly more time-consuming for the vendor and therefore the most costly of the options.

At the risk of injecting personal opinion into an otherwise objective article, I would have to say that Levels One through Three have the broadest applicability in the current environment. I fully believe that Levels Four and Five are workable options, and that vendors will rally and reorganize to meet the demand that develops. I do not advocate a future in which local selection has become the oddity rather than the norm. But perhaps a new area of specialty will develop—collection development librarians who work for vendors or who free-lance their services to more than one library. This may be in selection or in the broader arena of collection management, including evaluation. In any case, outsourcing of selection is not an all or nothing proposition. Each library can choose the levels of assistance that they need and with which they are most comfortable. I look forward to observing and participating in the next generation of vendor-assisted collection development services for public libraries.

REFERENCE

1. Robert D. Chapman, "The Review-Driven Purchase Plan at Detroit Public Library," *Against the Grain* (September 1, 1997): 86-88.

How the WLN Conspectus Works
for Small Libraries

Burns Davis

SUMMARY. In many ways small libraries have an advantage when using the conspectus method to assess their collections: assessment details are easier to manage and the entire conspectus picture is more readily visualized. This article looks at some of the benefits of using the conspectus in small libraries and suggests appropriate adaptions of the conspectus structure. WLN conspectus software is an efficient tool for assessing small collections in public libraries. The software flexibility enables librarians to produce customized assessment results by adapting the conspectus techniques and tools according to the arrangement of resources in local collections. The conspectus structure provides a standardized point of reference for quickly surveying and describing the entire range of a small library's resources. Information about library collections may be shared efficiently among collaborating libraries and their communities when information about collections is organized into an assessment using the conspectus method. *[Article copies available for a fee from The Haworth Document Delivery Service: 1-800-342-9678. E-mail address: getinfo@haworthpressinc.com]*

WHAT THE CONSPECTUS IS AND HOW IT IS USED

The Conspectus Concept

Collection assessment is an organized process for systematically describing a library's information resources at a particular point in time.

Burns Smith Davis is Information Resources Coordinator for the Nebraska Library Commission, 1200 N Street, Suite 120, Lincoln, NE 68508-2023.

[Haworth co-indexing entry note]: "How the WLN Conspectus Works for Small Libraries." Davis, Burns. Co-published simultaneously in *The Acquisitions Librarian* (The Haworth Press, Inc.) No. 20, 1998, pp. 53-72; and: *Public Library Collection Development in the Information Age* (ed: Annabel K. Stephens) The Haworth Press, Inc., 1998, pp. 53-72. Single or multiple copies of this article are available for a fee from The Haworth Document Delivery Service [1-800-342-9678, 9:00 a.m. - 5:00 p.m. (EST). E-mail address: getinfo@haworthpressinc.com].

53

Assessment evaluates the effectiveness of the library's collection in supporting the library's local purpose, and interprets the results as a statement of need or plan of action. It uses a set of quantitative measures and qualitative techniques to describe the resources in the library's collection. The resulting portrait of the collection is used to make management decisions. An assessment compares the existing information resources to the role of the library in order to determine in what ways the collection meets or fails the needs of clients. The anticipated outcome of collection assessment is a plan of action to manage the library's information resources.

The general approach to describing a collection of information resources is called an assessment. There are a number of ways to organize an assessment. One of the most widely used methods is that of conspectus. A conspectus is simply a brief survey or summary of a subject: an outline or a synopsis. The conspectus method enables librarians to compile data in a consistent way which records and displays that information according to standards that encourage collaborative comparisons regardless of physical arrangement or classification schemes. The conspectus structure becomes a common denominator for collection descriptions.[1]

The WLN conspectus structure divides the universe of knowledge into twenty-four divisions which are further subdivided by categories and subjects. The divisions are correlated on worksheets for Dewey or LC classification schedules. The conspectus structure and the software are adapted to all types and sizes of libraries in many parts of the world. Small libraries in school, public, and special library environments successfully practice assessment using the conspectus method.

Data Collection

The information collected should support the collection assessment steps of planning, data gathering, assigning collection indicators, and resource management decision making. The three data collection techniques that are most often used in an assessment are:

- title count
- median age
- shelf observation

The information gathered about the collection is used to describe the vital qualities of the library's resources. These qualities include:

- the collection's adequacy to support services
- formats/type of materials

- usage
- languages
- reading levels
- priorities and collecting responsibilities

Maintenance actions are determined from the assessment results. Common decisions relate to:

- weeding
- replacing
- updating
- adding
- preserving/conserving

The selection of what data to collect is determined by which portions of the collection have greatest priority to the library's mission, which items are the most numerous, which resources are most used by library customers, and which data are most relevant to the way assessment results will be used in decision making.

The many different techniques for evaluating collections may be divided into two groups–those that are primarily collection-centered and those that are more client-centered. Collection-centered techniques examine the content and characteristics of the information resources themselves in order to determine the size, age, scope, and depth of the collection in comparison to collection goals, an external standard, or the universe of possibilities. Client-centered techniques describe how the collection is used by patrons and indicate its effectiveness. Collection assessment results are likely to be most useful when a combination of client-centered and collection-centered techniques including both quantitative and qualitative results are employed in the data gathering and description process.

It is up to the individual librarian to determine exactly which methods will be used. This decision is based upon the availability of data, the amount of staff and other resources to be devoted to the assessment, and the way the assessment results are to be used within the library. The methods and techniques should be chosen during the planning stages of the assessment.

Some factors that should be considered when planning assessments are:

- shelflist order and cataloging
- shelf display
- reading level separations

- circulation counting procedures
- collection management policy selection criteria
- purchasing and weeding data record keeping procedures
- local library fiction subdivision terminology
- collection sub-units
- service objectives for fiction materials
- record keeping about program use

These elements influence how the conspectus will be adapted for assessment of a local library collection.[2]

The nature of each collection segment is described with a numerical collection depth indicator.[3] These indicators are defined from 1 through 5 in *Using the Conspectus Method: A Collection Assessment Handbook* (Bushing, Davis, & Powell, 1997). Examples of these indicators appear on the sample assessment reports from the example public library. The primary factors to consider in describing the collection are:

- The universe of publication and the scope of the division
- The library's collection in relation to holdings in other libraries
- Access to the collection
- Physical characteristics of the resources
- Use of the collection
- The nature of the subject literature and types of materials appropriate to the subject

The points to consider in reviewing the collection, noting significant features, and assigning collection depth indicators are the same for all areas of the collection, including fiction and special collection sections.

Data Reports

Assessment information reports are organized by WLN Conspectus® line numbers. The reports are printed in graph and text formats. Uniform notes in the WLN Conspectus® software comments field are searchable and topical reports can be printed from these notes. The reports generated from the notes entered in the comments field may be related to subjects that are important to local customers, collection management actions needed, or special materials formats. For example, searching the conspectus notes for assessment comments about "weeding" will produce a list of collection sections the librarian wants to weed. Other examples are subject-related reports for local history, or lists of resources of particular formats such as videos. The reports create the basic information for a librarian's decisions about collection maintenance actions. These reports are effective communication tools for presenting library information to boards, community groups, and faculty. Examples of terms from which useful reports may be produced by searching the conspectus notes are:

Audiocassettes
Curriculum Support
CD-ROMs
Local history
Update/Replace/Add
Videos
Weed

HOW THE CONSPECTUS IS DIFFERENT IN SMALL LIBRARIES

Small libraries have many advantages ahead of larger libraries in conducting an assessment. With few people involved and smaller numbers of resources it is simpler to control the project details and timeline. Because the assessment of a small library collection is compact in scope, the project can be completed within a short time frame. Librarians working with small collections can effectively complete shelf observation of their entire collections. A small-sized assessment also produces a succinct description of resources that is easily visualized. Special collections, unique features, and glaring oversights or anomalies stand out visibly on assessment reports. In a small library, an assessment can take full advantage of the range of conspectus flexibility without needing highly complicated adjustments to the assessment process and the software. The margin of data error in smaller assessments is relatively quite wide because it is easier to undo errors when working on a small scale, and it is easier to detect errors within a smaller framework. Resources in all formats in a small library can be included in a clear, simple way. The condensed range of resources permits librarians in small libraries to develop tightly focused collection management plans, making it possible for them to quickly improve the general effectiveness of the collection. Clients, administrative body, and staff are readily aware of the assessment project, its progress, its results, and its impact. Public support may help a librarian to achieve progress toward goals for a more effective collection.

SPECIAL BENEFITS FOR SMALL LIBRARIES

The conspectus method is a standardized way of quickly surveying and describing the entire range of a library's resources. The uniform terminology and structure make it possible for librarians to easily share information about their collections because the data about the collection is grouped by subject, independent of classification schedules or types of formats. The conspectus is a standardized foundation for surveying and describing resources in all formats. It is an especially useful way to incorporate electronic resources and uncataloged groups of materials into assessment of the library's entire body of resources.

Any variety of special collection groupings can be included in the assessment. At the same time, unique features stand out for quick recognition. Any variety of specialized services for local patrons can also be featured in special reports. There is great flexibility in the conspectus method which permits every project to be planned to suit the local library and its available staff. Assessment projects can be customized for each library. Training and data collection can be tailored to each library's needs. Volunteers can help as members of the assessment team.

Prepared conspectus reports give a communication edge for a small library. The assessment results are organized in presentations that have professional polish and credibility with the library's public, especially with funding officials, who need documentation and statistical data to support budget requests. The conspectus method relates resources to service delivery in a standardized presentation format. The format of assessment results presents facts about resource use and performance in easily visualized graph styles. Spreadsheet presentations of conspectus data are familiar counterparts to frequently used business tools.

METHODS

Assessing the entire collection with all formats, special groupings, and reading levels is much more achievable in a small library than in large libraries. During an assessment, information is compiled about the quality and quantity of information materials. The primary methods used to collect information about the collection are shelf list measurement, shelf observation, and usage data. Using the WLN Conspectus® is especially helpful for assessing areas of a collection that contain significant groups of unclassified materials. Collections of specialized items, for example cake pans or puppets, may be popular items in circulation. Often these are not classified or cataloged. Therefore, they would not show up on an inventory list. However, information about these items could be easily shared with another library as part of conspectus-based assessment reports. Unique local history collections and specialized collection strengths are other examples of collection data that are most easily handled with the conspectus method. Using the conspectus allows the library to assess the collection by subject areas regardless of the classification scheme or unclassified status of resources.

Librarians obtain accurate, descriptive information about the character, size, age, and general quality of their present resources from an assessment. Conspectus reports communicate what the library does not now have, and what it intends to have in the future. Data organized in the conspectus structure facilitate resource sharing. Assessing a library collection produces as accurate a picture as possible of what resources the library has to support its service to customers. The conspectus reports facilitate complementary resource management between libraries.

HOW IT CAN WORK

Documentation of the assessment has many uses. It is used in collection management, correlation and updating of the library's Collection Development Policy, developing action for curriculum support, documentation to support the annual budget, and disaster preparedness.

The conspectus offers a great deal of flexibility in collecting and recording data. There are many possible ways to customize conspectus structure. It is necessary to carefully choose only what is important to know and eliminate all else. Since most librarians will have very little time to prepare for an assessment, the time spent needs to produce relevant results quickly.

Organizing data collection and reports into sections that correlate to the library's own customer groups helps librarians to see what the supply of materials is in relation to their usage. This is especially easy to do in a small library using the possibilities built into the conspectus method and software. Some of the options for customizing the conspectus are the creating of local divisions, defining macros for search terms in notes, adding searchable comments in notes fields, customizing spreadsheet data collection, designing the assessment process to local conditions, and using the management information file to collect acquisitions data. Any unique categories that are appropriate for local customer service may be accommodated in the conspectus without eroding the validity of the assessment structure and results.

CONCLUSIONS THAT CAN BE DRAWN
FROM ASSESSMENT OBSERVATIONS

During interpretation of the assessment results, the most important overall characteristic is that the collection should appear generally consistent with the selection objectives expressed in the library policy statement. Forming a plan of action for collection management is the desired outcome of the assessment process. Planning for sufficient numbers of current materials for general circulation and reference service, and developing the proposed areas of program or curriculum support will probably be key points in the action plan.

Follow up to the assessment accomplishes the following objectives:

- Check the median age of reference categories and additional specialized areas of the collection for currency.
- Update information which has high circulation and for which the median age is older than appropriate for the subject.
- Assign preservation commitments for maintaining materials and preserving content.
- Plan maintenance strategies of weeding and purchasing for continuing collection development.
- Use assessment information in interlibrary collaboration.
- Share the information with community and staff.

HOW USE OF THE CONSPECTUS FITS
INTO SMALL LIBRARY OPERATIONS

Some basic uses of collection assessment results are the preparation of an acquisitions plan, weeding plan, and budget. The results form the basis of collection management performance evaluation and document supporting information for collaborative agreements.

Using Conspectus Results to Develop
a Collection Management Action Plan

Reports from the assessment are used to check the goal levels against what is currently in the collection and to target subject divisions where there are differences in these levels for development in the action plan. These differences are easy to see in the report graphs. The assessment comments printed in the report texts may suggest items for the action plan. This plan will be developed by a local librarian with involvement, as appropriate, of the library staff, board, and community. An effective action plan includes the subject areas to be developed, number of titles needed, desired formats, reading levels, and estimated costs.

An acquisitions plan includes a budget for books, periodicals, CDs, videos, electronic resources, and other formats. It states the number of materials needed, estimated cost, means of acquisition–purchase, donation, cooperative purchase–and space needed for shelving and computer access or in-house use.

A weeding plan is developed that will move low-use materials out of the library collection or out of key traffic areas and keep materials of recent median age within ready shelf access. A conservative estimation of annual weeding is 5-7 percent of the total collection.

Using Conspectus Results to Develop a Budget

A library's budget is a communication tool as well as a planning instrument. Conspectus assessment effectively presents easily-assimilated facts about a library's resources which can be used as supporting information for a library's budget. The following significant points of information are readily formatted in the conspectus:

- Proportions of materials related to general collection management objectives.
- Special or local interest collections.
- Reading interests.
- Numerical goals for checking collection management progress.
- Amounts needed for building resources in popular interests, hot topics, and underrepresented subjects.
- Proportionate priorities for program areas.
- Specific client groups.

Conspectus reports can provide numerical goals for checking progress that concern funding bodies and librarians alike. Numerical goals may be expressed as numbers of titles, volumes, or dollar amounts. Ways to effectively use conspectus assessment results with a library budget include:

- Provide budget documentation supporting the library's annual statistical reports and long range plan.

- Present reports, collect operations data, and evaluate progress in a manner organized consistently with the budgeting and accounting principles used by the library.
- Estimate costs from the average price of various formats in targeted subject areas.
- Present relevant documentation in a way that is understandable by the major groups which work with the library: community, staff, board, friends, government, special populations, and accreditation bodies.
- Select timing for collection management activities that is coordinated with the library's budget cycle.
- Plan reassessment data to evaluate progress.

Conspectus reports are particularly useful in supporting the factual information presented in the library's budget. Demonstrations of desirable collection conditions can be strengthened with comparison reports from other libraries. A librarian's budgeting responsibility is to identify all the pertinent factors that need to be considered in preparing the budget, to determine correct proportions for expenditures based on the collection management policy and collection depth indicators for collection goals, and to develop meaningful forecasting techniques for planning proactive resource changes to keep in step with format and subject trends. A certain amount of budgeting activity is the reporting of actual expenditures and resource acquisitions in comparison to the budgeted dollar and title amounts. Progress can be readily visualized using the comparison reports from successive conspectus assessments. A librarian's skill in projecting trends and planning for them is measured partly by budget performance.

Common factors to consider in preparing public library budgets include:

- Trends in publishing
  - New formats
  - Cost increases, decreases
  - Availability of formats and new subject resources
  - Popular subjects, consumer affairs, and research developments of interest to the library's customers
- The library's planned development of subject areas, formats, and special collections
- The library's commitment to core collection resources of reference, fiction, and nonfiction
- The library's commitment to customer service groups, reading interest groups, and special populations

Line item budgets which are still used by some libraries are effectively supported with documentation from conspectus reports. However, program-related, or service objective budgets which are more in use today are particularly well-supported by conspectus reports which can document progress from one assessment period to the next. Regardless of the type of budget used by a library, conspectus reports are excellent planning instruments which clearly express the current collection status as well as the commitment to acquisitions goals. Assessment reports effectively communicate expenditure plans in relation to program objectives.

Using Conspectus Results to Evaluate Collection Management Performance

Collection management often occurs in a void where there is little documentation of measurable results. Additions and withdrawals from the collection are usually recorded as numbers of titles, volumes, and dollars spent. Similar information is often kept about formats and service areas, such as reference or children's services. Libraries less often collect information about collection management activities in a manner which organizes data about purchasing and discarding activity by subjects in a way that relates these facts to management and service goals, and is kept current on a daily or weekly basis. Proportions of format and genre holdings can be related to service areas in a picture of the overall effectiveness of collection management activities toward reaching a library's goals. The Management Information File is the WLN Conspectus® software file where ongoing acquisitions and weeding information is entered. Reports from this file organize this data in conspectus order which means that up-to-date collection management activity is readily available in subject-related reports.

A library's first collection assessment establishes the benchmark against which future progress will be measured. Over time, changes in a library's resources will be mapped on successive assessment reports. A useful history is built of increasing resource effectiveness or decreasing ability to support library services. This information contributes to decision making and program justification by providing a methodical, uniform structure for comparing management expectations with real achievement in practice. For a one-person library, completing a conspectus-based assessment gives a librarian an effective tool for efficient, self-directed work organization, and a standardized means of communicating facts about the library collection.

Using Conspectus Results to Develop a Collaborative Agreement

Knowing what is available in each partner library's collection is an important starting point for collaboration between libraries. To develop a collaborative agreement, comparison of resource access needs to take place within a commonly-shared structure that equalizes classification schedules, uncataloged resources, automated catalogs or shelf lists, and varied material formats. Data flexibility and customizing increase the amount of communication that can take place between the collaborating libraries. Using the conspectus tool will solidly support the process of identifying and comparing what each partner has. Points of agreement about responsibilities and expectations can be related to specific subject areas in the written conspectus notes, with great flexibility for changing and reporting decisions. This statement of mutual objectives is readily available to all partners for updating and sharing. The conspectus documentation serves as an aid to finding resources within the partnership. Each group of clients served by the individual partner libraries benefits from the strength of this collection-building collaboration.

SOME CONSIDERATIONS ESPECIALLY IMPORTANT TO SMALL LIBRARIES

Fiction collections are important resources especially in small- and medium-sized public libraries where fiction materials may be the busiest and most numerous materials in the library. In a public library it is possible for the fiction collection to represent half or more of the total resources, and fiction materials may comprise 50 percent or more of the library's circulation.[4] It is particularly important that helpful alternatives are available for libraries to assess their fiction materials. Libraries often do not use classification schedules to organize fiction, choosing instead to arrange materials in units related to the way their customers look for them.[5] Fiction materials are commonly shelved in genre, format, or reading level sections which are organized alphabetically by authors' names. These sections tend to be much like the genre and format arrangements found in commercial book stores.[6]

Non-book materials, periodicals, recordings, video, CD-ROM, and audio book formats may be located in uncataloged groupings arranged by title or type of use. These materials may be heavily used, or support curriculum and programs, and should be included in an assessment.

An example of this kind of uncataloged material is a library's vertical file which can be an important resource for reference and school reports. Notes may be added in the assessment report in the relevant conspectus location about the total number of pieces, subjects available, what types of use the file supports, and the nature of materials included. In conspectus divisions where the vertical file is a significant resource, notes can be included in the comments field of the conspectus worksheet. A median age of the materials could be obtained by sampling.

Comparing Resources

How do small libraries find useful comparisons for determining the universe of publication against which a collection is measured? Size is largely independent of the determination of collection effectiveness. The concepts of relative collection development are defined as collection depth indicators 1 through 5 in *Using the Conspectus Method: A Collection Assessment Handbook.*[7] Visiting other library collections and browsing bookstores, online catalogs, and trade journals are useful ways to keep up with publishing activity. Evaluations of a library's collection depth are based upon comparisons of a library's resources to the publications available in a subject. There is no standardized numerical formula of how many resources a library should provide. However, a library's conspectus-based collection assessment is a highly effective document in which the collection's effectiveness in meeting service objectives is expressed in observation comments and collection depth indicators.

Planning, Training, and Data Collection

Training time for a review of collection management principles, basic conspectus methods, and instructions in data collection techniques can be greatly condensed for a small library. Initial data evaluation takes place at the end of data collection. Assistance from experienced assessors will help a librarian to implement an efficient assessment. Planning, training, data collection design, data interpretation, and preparation of reports are several functions which an experienced assessor can facilitate. Help using the WLN conspectus may also be beneficial. People who might help may be library collection management consultants, state library staff, other public librarians, university librarians, systems librarians, or WLN staff. WLN is a good referral source for locating librarians who are knowledgeable about conspectus practice in small libraries. Some state libraries and consortia provide significant training, consulting, data entry, and software support for libraries undergoing assessment.

Data collection can take as long as is allowed. A reasonable time frame can be planned by deciding by what date the data will be used and how much time can be spent working on the project. In the following example, volunteer staff were added to the public library assessment teams to make it possible to complete the data collection in four days. The entire assessment including training, data collection, basic data interpretation, and printed conspectus reports was concluded within the week.

Special Collections and Subject or Reading Interest Groupings

Reviewing the assessment results with the space allocated for library activities is useful for checking the adequacy of space in new or existing facilities. Space in relation to support priorities is particularly important for the following three types of areas:

1. The staff work areas and storage spaces. Areas allotted for materials processing, staff work activities, computer work stations, and periodical shelving should reflect the relative importance of these activities in providing resources to support a library's service objectives.
2. Collection shelving allowance. Projections of space needed for volumes in the current collection and the addition of an adequate number of titles for children and general circulation to meet collecting goals can be specifically based on the collection action plan for purchasing and weeding.
3. Reading, study, and computer access areas for customers. If these spaces are reduced to allow for shelving expansion, customer service may be affected adversely. Floor plans should be carefully reviewed to consider adequate space for all types of customer usage and for adequate housing of an appropriate number of materials to serve customers.

There may be other important aspects regarding space needs. The space design should be evaluated in relation to the library's program priorities and the resources used, as clearly stated in the collection assessment report.

Local Adaptions of the Conspectus Structure

In some libraries materials with special characteristics or formats are grouped together. These may be organized as juvenile, fiction, biography, large print, or discipline-specific collections. All parts of the collection, including local special collections, are characterized in an assessment in order to aid continuing collection management. Specific adaptions of the conspectus can produce customized reports about local special collections if terms are added in the comments field during data collection.

Collection assessment is usually accomplished using a combination of techniques that generate both quantitative measures and qualitative descriptors of the existing information resources. The most frequently used measures include, but are not limited to: title count, age, format, and use statistics; direct examination of the collection (shelf-scanning); list and citation checking; and evaluation by an outside expert. Flexibility of the conspectus method provides the opportunity to utilize local quantitative data and to tailor the process to the staff available for the project. Special aspects of the collection that relate to local service patterns and outstanding areas of the library materials collection may be profiled in reports or interdisciplinary divisions. This may be accomplished by assessing selected subjects within existing divisions, by adding local divisions to the conspectus, or by adding uniform notes in the WLN Conspectus® comments field.

A locally created division presents the data for special collections at the level of other divisions, keeping the relative importance of all materials equal in supporting library service delivery to customers. Data about these specialized materials can then be manipulated utilizing the full range of features of the WLN Conspectus® software for showing the data on printed results in text and graph reports. The reporting options are somewhat more limited if data is handled in interdisciplinary divisions or in the searchable comments field.

Local divisions with any necessary categories and subjects may be added to the WLN Conspectus® in order to reflect a library's usage of these materials. Possible local divisions with their category and subject headings are shown in the following public library example. The example shows categories which reflect shelf arrangements and subjects defined by genres.

A PUBLIC LIBRARY EXAMPLE

Here is an example of how an assessment project adapted the conspectus method to fit a public library which serves a community of 9,700. The desired outcome was to show what curriculum support materials are available and what will be needed, what resources in volumes and dollars will be needed to develop the collection, how well the space allowed in a new building will be used, and what weeding can be done in the collection.

The entire library collection was assessed including uncataloged and cataloged resources in all formats and all reading levels. Information about the collection was gathered from shelf observation, usage data, and shelflist measurement. In general, the collection was assessed at the division level. Children's nonfiction materials are intershelved with adult materials and were assessed in the standard conspectus lines. Outstanding areas of the collection that relate to local service patterns were profiled either by assessing selected categories or subjects within divisions, by adding local divisions to the conspectus, or by adding uniform notes in the WLN Conspectus® comments field. Adding a quick note to the conspectus line as assessors located relevant materials during shelf observation proved to be an effective way to identify materials related to local history and curriculum support. These materials are partially shelved as a unit, but most are scattered throughout this collection. Reports were printed from these notes. Three types of reports were used: reports about resources in special formats or about specific services, reports about collection development action to be taken, and reports about customer use.

The locally created divisions for this library match service categories of high-use sections of the collection such as fiction items. In this library these divisions include many unclassified and uncataloged materials and nonprint formats. Several of the customized divisions are listed here as examples of possible local adaptions to the conspectus.[8]

DIVISION/*Category*/Subject

ADULT FICTION
  Adult Fiction
    Adventure
    General
    Mystery
    Romance
    Science Fiction and Fantasy
    Horror
    Western
    Historical
  Adult Paperback Rack
    General fiction
    Novels
    Miscellaneous
    Romance
    Western
  Audio Books

HOLIDAY

JUVENILE FICTION

Juvenile Fiction General
Juvenile Paperback
Juvenile Easy
Easy Cassettes

REFERENCE

Agriculture reference
Anthropology reference
Art and Architecture reference
Biological Sciences reference
Business and Economics reference
Chemistry reference
Computer Sciences reference
Education reference
Engineering and Technology reference
Geography and Earth Sciences reference
Language, Linguistics, and Literature reference
Law reference
Library Science and Generalities reference
Mathematics reference
Medicine reference
Performing Arts reference
Philosophy and Religion reference
Physical Education and Recreation reference
Physical Science reference
Political Science reference
Psychology reference
Sociology reference

During the assessment process shelf list date sampling and shelf observation techniques were also adapted to verify median age with use in a high circulation per item environment. The flexibility of the conspectus software and the resilience of the assessment techniques enabled us to adapt the conspectus structure as necessary for the local environment and to still produce a valid and thorough assessment for this small library. Data from this library can be compared with other libraries' results in the WLN database.

The assessment results from this example library confirmed that collection maintenance is taking place and also pointed out areas where older materials remain on shelves. Assessment reports identified key areas that need updating and weeding, allowing the librarian to plan budget requests and collection maintenance activities before the move to the new library. The librarian began using the assessment results immediately to set weeding priorities and to estimate space needs for moving the collection to a new facility. The librarian will also use the assessment results to plan the most effective shelving arrangement in the new space. The uses of space in the proposed new building were reviewed on the construction plans to determine if there is adequate shelf room, if there are potential physical hazards to library materials, and if the space layouts are well-arranged for public access and service.

The purposes of performing an assessment in this library were to describe the status of the collection and to collect data that would support a budget plan for developing the library's resources. As the shelf observations were taking place during the assessment project, staff were identifying sections that need selecting and weeding attention. These observations were collected and reported in the searchable comments field of the WLN Conspectus®. The assessment reports were used by the library staff and library board as supporting documentation to explain budget requests and building needs to the City Council and the community. Other areas that will support community college curriculum and student study will benefit from the action plan developed by the librarian for purchasing materials in those subject areas.

The librarian, who regularly attends to her collection's maintenance by selecting new materials and weeding, knows her community thoroughly and has many years of service experience in this library. Her statement about the project summed the assessment benefits very well:

> I learned so much about the collection. It [the assessment] really gave me a better idea about what to DO![9]

CONCLUSION

Choosing an assessment approach that adapts the conspectus structure to local library practice is useful for organizing assessment information about resources in the collection that are arranged by:

- specialized local interest
- format
- genre
- usage (customer group)

Resources typically arranged in these kinds of units are often not classified by Dewey or Library of Congress schedules. These local groupings are practical relationships that usually reflect something about the service delivery given by the library. Types of materials often handled in functional subdivisions are:

- fiction
- biography
- biographical fiction
- nonprint formats
- local interest collections
- children's materials
- adaptive formats such as large type

The innate flexibility of the conspectus method enables librarians who assess small collections to customize assessment procedures. A choice may be made from locally created divisions, interdisciplinary divisions, and reports generated from searchable comments. Small libraries use assessment results to form acquisitions plans and weeding plans, to calculate cost projections and compile budgets, to evaluate collection management performance, and to form collaborative agreements. A smaller scope is an advantage for assessing library collections in a method that reflects local library service patterns. Assessing librarians are encouraged to adapt the conspectus and assessment project methods to suit their local needs.

REFERENCES

1. Mary Bushing, Burns Davis and Nancy Powell. *Using the Conspectus Method: A Collection Assessment Handbook.* (Lacey, WA: WLN, 1997), 21.

2. Burns Davis, "Using Local Marketing Characteristics to Customize the Conspectus for Fiction Assessment," *The Acquisitions Librarian* [In press 1998], 10.

3. Mary Bushing et al., 28-31.

4. Burns Davis, 4.

5. Davis, Burns. "Designing a Fiction Assessment Tool: The Customer Service Approach." In Georgine N. Olson and Barbara McFadden Allen, Eds. *Cooperative Collection Management: The Conspectus Approach.* New York: Neal-

Schuman Publishers, Inc., 1994, 78-79. [Special issue of *Collection Building* (1994), 13: 2-3.]

6. Baker, Sharon L. *The Responsive Public Library Collection: How to Develop and Market It.* (Englewood, CO: Libraries Unlimited, Inc., 1993).

7. Mary Bushing et al., 28-31.

8. Burns Davis, 13-14.

9. Ibid., 18.

Collection Development in the Information Age: Great Britain's Public Libraries

Joy M. Greiner

SUMMARY. This article describes three public libraries in the United Kingdom: Croydon, Dunfermline, and York. The objective was to describe the different levels of technology in these libraries and the steps that are being taken to move them into the 21st century. The effects of community and user input were topics of interest. The history of the development of the individual libraries or systems as well as the current organizational structures are described. Government unitary authority changes affects two of the three libraries. Unique characteristics of each of the libraries are emphasized. Research was conducted over a two year period and includes interviews, observations, and secondary sources. The intent is not to compare the libraries, but to illustrate how the varying levels of automation affect patron resources and services. *[Article copies available for a fee from The Haworth Document Delivery Service: 1-800-342-9678. E-mail address: getinfo@haworthpressinc.com]*

INTRODUCTION

This paper is the result of an investigation to examine the effect of technology on the collection development policies and processes in se-

Joy M. Greiner is Director at the School of Library and Information Science, University of Southern Mississippi, Southern Station Box 5146, Hattiesburg, MS 39406.

[Haworth co-indexing entry note]: "Collection Development in the Information Age: Great Britain's Public Libraries." Greiner, Joy M. Co-published simultaneously in *The Acquisitions Librarian* (The Haworth Press, Inc.) No. 20, 1998, pp. 73-89; and: *Public Library Collection Development in the Information Age* (ed: Annabel K. Stephens) The Haworth Press, Inc., 1998, pp. 73-89. Single or multiple copies of this article are available for a fee from The Haworth Document Delivery Service [1-800-342-9678, 9:00 a.m. - 5:00 p.m. (EST). E-mail address: getinfo@haworthpressinc.com].

73

lected public libraries in Great Britain. Three libraries were chosen, two in England and one in Scotland. Each of the libraries had been visited prior to the 1997 study. The intent of the paper is to describe the current use of technology and its effect on services provided in each of the libraries, not to compare the libraries with each other.

The Croydon Central Library, located in a South Borough of London, was selected as the result of a visit in the summer 1996. The Croydon Library had been recommended as an outstanding example of an innovative community information and cultural resource by the British coordinator for the *Libraries and Museums* course offered by the University of Southern Mississippi's British Studies Program.

When the York Library, in the ancient northern city of York, England, was first visited by the researcher in 1994, it was part of the North Yorkshire County Libraries System. This system was identified as one of the largest regional public library systems in England. After the Unitary Authority changes, this library became head of the City of York Libraries.

The Dunfermline Central Library is located in Dunfermline, Scotland, the birthplace of Andrew Carnegie. The original library opened to the public on August 29, 1863 and represented the beginning of Carnegie's library philanthropy, the topic being researched by the author during a 1995 visit.

RELATED LITERATURE

In 1988, George R. Jaramillo, Associate Professor of Library Science at the University of Northern Colorado, described the projected effect of computer technology on collection development and the role of the professional librarian. He defined the collection "as a profile of the needs and interests of its users."[1] Jaramillo asserted that nonprofessionals could take over the duties of operating a centralized acquisitions and cataloguing network, and that "ordering, receipt, cataloguing and routing of materials can be accomplished with little or no professional involvement."[2]

Jaramillo cited Wilfred Lancaster's identification of the three major functions of a library as selection and acquisition, organization and control, and provision of various services. Lancaster asserted that

> in a largely electronic world, the first two functions decline substantially in importance. Electronic sources, at least those remotely accessible, do not need to be acquired, nor do they need selection. . . . librarians select what to access to satisfy a known demand rather than what to purchase in anticipation of future demands.[3]

James Thompson identified a new role that needs to be taken by librarians in collection development if libraries are to survive. In 1982, he projected that librarians would be builders of links between users and the computer age.[4]

Mary E. Jackson, in a 1994 survey of the use of technology in selected urban public libraries in the United States, focused on eight broad service areas that were enhanced by the creative use of technology. Three of these dealt specifically with library collections: improving access to the library's collection, access to remote materials and collections, and increasing the use of collections.[5] Jackson concluded that the use of technology allowed professional librarians to focus on technical and policy issues while library technicians filled technical service positions.[6]

Information Technology in Public Libraries described the results of the fifth of the surveys conducted over a period of ten years by Chris Batt, Borough Libraries and Museums Officer, London Borough of Croydon. The studies examined the development of information technology in public libraries in Great Britain. Library management systems, electronic information services, and micros for the public and for the staff were the areas investigated through a questionnaire. The 100 percent response rate[7] to the 1993 questionnaire shows that of the 168 library authorities in the UK, 137 or 82% had automated circulation systems.[8] In 1993, 144 respondents had automated catalogue production, either integrated with circulation,[9] local mainframe data processing,[10] or agency service.[11] The catalogue was available online (staff only) in 57 of the authorities, online (public) in 83, on fiche/film in 75, and hardcopy in 30 in 1993. The most dramatic increase was in online (public) from 7 in 1985 to 83 in 1993.[12] Automated acquisitions was reported in 111 of the authorities. Of these, 81 were integrated with circulation, 32 with a direct link to the supplier, 7 with an inhouse micro, 15 with an inhouse mini/mframe, and 8 reported "other."[13]

Batt, in his introduction to the fifth edition of *Information Technology in Public Libraries,* asked the provocative question, "Does information technology matter?" He went on to make a distinction between the individual needs of managers and what library services are about.[14] He referred to the government review that would redraw boundary maps and create a larger number of unitary authorities, and to the decisions that would need to be made in regard to technology.[15]

Batt mentioned that public libraries in the United States had a strong history of network awareness, and noted that he had visited libraries in the United States well ahead of the United Kingdom in the use of information technology, but he had also visited US public libraries without basic technology, such as a telephone. He described the situation in the UK where there are library authorities without library management systems, CD-ROM, online searching, or some other common applications of technology. He noted that in some library systems, technology applications may be available in only one or two branches. Small, remote rural libraries may not be connected at all. He added that there are no libraries where online searching is provided at every service point.[16]

METHODOLOGY

Discussions in each of the libraries for the current study focused on the extent and specific role of automation in collection development and accessibility. The automated systems in place or planned, the software used, library operations that were already automated, the number of public access terminals, customer and staff access to the Internet, community involvement in the choice of materials, and the role of censorship in collection building were the areas examined.

Interviews were conducted with library administrators at various levels in each of the libraries. Brenda Constable, Central Library Manager, and Frank Edwards, Resources and Technical Services Manager, participated in interviews and provided interesting and worthwhile information about the Croydon Borough Libraries. *Information Technology in Public Libraries,* by Chris Batt, Libraries and Museums Officer for the Croydon Central Library, was a valuable resource.

In the summer of 1997, Pat Anderson, the Acting Chief of the Dunfermline District Libraries and West Area Libraries, discussed the current status and vision for the future of this historic library. Anne Rodwell, local history librarian, and Sally Joice, librarian for lending libraries, provided information about their particular areas of involvement.

Ellen Hamblett, stock librarian in the City of York library, discussed the changes in the structure of public libraries in Great Britain, specifically in the Yorkshire District Libraries. The implications for library operations and services were discussed in an informative interview.

Reorganization of government agencies into new unitary authorities in England and Scotland began in 1996, and was still being implemented at the time of the researcher's visit. As a result, many library systems have been restructured. In some cases, large systems have divided into a number of smaller systems, and conversely, single library districts have merged with other districts to form one centralized system.

The public libraries in the study are governed directly by elected officials. There is not a library Board of Trustees, usually appointed by the elected officials, as is the case in the United States. One librarian commented that direct authority by elected officials was an example of democracy in action: the officials were elected by the people, and as such, they governed the libraries that served the people.

CROYDON CENTRAL LIBRARY

Background

The new Croydon Central Library was formally opened November 5, 1993, during National Library Week by Heritage Secretary Peter Brooke. In his remarks, Brooke noted that this library was the largest new public library built in the UK for many years.[17]

The library is part of the Clocktower development and includes the historic Town Hall, a museum, exhibition galleries, cinema, cafe, theatre, and tourist information center and gift shop. The development involved the refurbishment of the Victorian Town Hall, originally opened by the then Prince of Wales (later King Edward VII)[18] in May 1896; the building of a new library, and the creation of the museum and arts complex. The approximate cost of this unique project was 30 million pounds.[19] The magnificent landmark Clocktower dominates the view, while the statue of Queen Victoria to the right of the entrance to the culture centre celebrates the blending of the traditional and the modern. The library was described in a newspaper article as "Cyberspace in a Victorian setting."[20]

Governed directly by the 70 elected councilors, the libraries and museum complex serves a population of 320,000. The Council raises a local community charge tax to supplement monies received from the central government, and all library monies are channeled through the Council. There are twelve library branches in addition to the Central Library and a mobile library. This state-of-the-art public library offers Internet, CD-ROM and PC terminals.

The Customer Charter for the Croydon Libraries Museum and Arts is available in the form of a flyer to all customers, and states in part that we intend to:

- make every reasonable effort to provide you with books, information and other items if, for reasons of age or disability, you are unable to use the central or branch libraries;
- buy sufficient numbers of books and other items to provide reasonable coverage of subjects, for general interest, recreational reading and study purposes;

- stock vocational and professional material for which there is sufficient demand;
- supply within 21 days at least 75% of books requested which are in Croydon Public Libraries current stock and provide information about your request when asked;
- provide access through the inter-library lending scheme, wherever possible, to any other book you might care to request;
- respond to 99% of your reference enquiries within two working days, by providing a comprehensive reference and information service at each library, both from its own stock of basic reference works and from immediate access to the reference and information services of the central library;
- provide comment forms for your use at each service point; and to respond to all comments where a reply has been requested;
- carry out regular surveys of customer satisfaction, and use the results in the planning of service.[21]

Interview Data

Frank Edwards, Resources and Technical Services Manager, in an interview reported that their target is to thru put all materials received within five days, but that they were actually doing 80 percent of receipts in two days, and urgent requests in 24 hours. Books are received from the supplier fully processed with bibliographic and item data. The library cataloguing system is GEAC, but the system for acquisitions and accounting is a stand alone system, Automated Library Systems International (ALSI). The ALSI system was chosen for the data out of inventory process to allow for efficient coordination of acquisitions and accounting. Its Electronic Data Information (EDI) capability enabled the department to trade electronically and gain additional discounts from book suppliers.

Edwards described the process as follows: Data resources managers manipulate the data. A week prior to receipt of a new title, bibliographic data in MARC format with Library of Congress (LC) subheadings is received at the library. This is loaded into the Potential Requirements Datafile (PRD) within the ALSI acquisitions system to form the basis of the order records. It is also loaded into the GEAC Library Management system to form the base record for the library catalogue and stock file.

Products are received in the central acquisitions department which adds the unique control number, format (book, audio, video, etc.), circulation rules, stock category, price, and agency to the stock record. For the majority of book materials, this is achieved by a batch-loading process using data created by suppliers. Thus several hundred books can be receipted and recorded in the stock file and catalogued within a few minutes. The product is received at the 14 service points, fully processed and with full bibliographic data, ready for immediate circulation to library customers.

Edwards said that 40 to 45 percent of the Resources (bibliographic) Services budget was allocated for data control and acquisitions functions, and that the department had six fulltime equivalent pure acquisitions staff members plus 16 1/2 fulltime equivalent staff overall. Data control operations and staff included the switchboard, technical services, collection management, and the stock editor. Edwards noted that the management and staff were involved in the fourth major change within the past fifteen years, requiring ongoing staff retraining and a flexible management style.

According to Edwards, Croydon had not been affected by the reorganization of local government. The reorganization only affected the counties and the larger towns included in them. He went on to say that it was too early to tell if the national change of government from Conservative to New Labour would have an effect. He noted that the new government had made some positive statements regarding public libraries' cultural and educational roles, and had set an objective for every library to have access to the Internet. The manner of funding has not been detailed.

When asked about the copyright issue, Edwards said that they alerted the staff and public to the law and any practices that were illegal. He added that Prentice Hall, a main publisher of book/CD-ROM products, and of books on disk, had issued them a license to loan. Prior to this, purchasing had been restricted by the licensing limitations imposed by the publisher (e.g., the first user to break the seal to the CD-ROM is deemed to be the sole user). The license to loan issued by Prentice Hall has been extended to all UK public libraries.

In addition to the ALSI purchasing system for order and receipting of new stock, Croydon has the Croydon's Library Management Computer System, CD-ROM and Online databases, and an Internet Web site which provides community information, bulletin board, e-mail and much more.

Croydon's public libraries have used computer systems to record the issue and return of stock since 1979. There was one VDU at the Central Library, and 40 barcode readers in the branches. Data were processed on a mainframe in the Council Information Technology section. In 1989 the CLSI LIBS 100 system was installed. This system recorded circulation and allowed staff to track reserved books and find out what books were on the shelf or on loan. It also flagged borrowers who had items overdue, included an online public access catalogue, and allowed the library to produce its own reports, statistics and overdue notices.

A new system was installed in the new Central Library in 1993. This was LIBS 100 Plus, developed by CLSI, which was bought by GEAC. This system is shared by the public libraries, two Colleges, and Schools Advisory Service (education resource centre). The management computer system networks 175 terminals and PCs at 17 sites across a star network. It provides a database with 260,000 title records in Machine Readable Catalogue (MARC) format, including author, title, control number, comprehensive subject headings and shelf location code; 770,000 item records, and 260,000 borrower records.

It includes a circulation module which records issue, return and renewal of library items, tracks reservations, alerts staff to overdue items and fines, and produces overdue notices and reports.

The system provided reservations information, a backup PC package which runs circulation functions when the online system is not available, and the "CL-CAT" public access catalogue which offers keyword and browse search capabilities for customers. Local and borough-wide library stock are displayed, showing where copies are shelved and whether they are in or on loan.

A public libraries user survey is conducted annually, and a flyer soliciting "compliments, comments, complaints" is available in the library. A personal reply is offered if persons will include name, address, and phone number. The user survey examines the reason(s) the customer came to the library (books, information, cassette(s), CD(s) or video(s)), the frequency of library visits, the level of satisfaction with the library, and demographics (age, gender, ethnicity, and occupation).

Brenda Constable, Central Library Manager, in response to a question about censorship said that anything published legally was acceptable. She added that there are stock selection guidelines, and the children's materials are carefully considered. Some books may be placed in the young adult section and in the adult library. She said that the current Carnegie Medal book is not in the children's collection but in the adult location. An extensive bibliography of gay and lesbian materials is available.

The Croydon libraries emphasize lifelong learning and information skills, and consider them basic skills. Customer services available at the Central Library during the researcher's visit included a CD-ROM for hire and 5 PCs for hire with word processing and spreadsheet software packages. WordPerfect for Windows and Microsoft for Windows were available for word processing, and Lotus 123 for Windows and Microsoft

Excel for Windows for spreadsheets. Two terminals provided public access to the Internet at a charge of 5 pounds for one hour or 2.50 pounds for concessions (seniors). These services were being made available to the public at some of the branch libraries at the time.

Information for Business in Croydon (IBC) is a member of the national Business Information Network; the information partner in Croydon Business Link; and an European Public Information relay centre. IBC is a local business information service that offers information free of charge on all aspects of business.

Batt, when discussing electronic information systems in *Information Technology in Public Libraries,* estimated that in Croydon

> including maintenance, staff time and the purchase of CD-ROMs, etc., we probably spend about 40,000 pounds a year; a figure which I suspect is at the high end of the expenditure range for public libraries in this country. By comparison we spend about 140,000 pounds each year on our library management system.[22]

DUNFERMLINE PUBLIC LIBRARY

Background

The building for the first Carnegie Free Library was donated to the citizens of Dunfermline, Scotland by Andrew Carnegie, who was born and lived there until he left with his family when he was nearly 14 years old. Carnegie offered to finance the new library in 1879 with the condition that the Town Council would adopt the Free Library Act of 1867. The Council complied with Carnegie's requirement in February 1880, and the first Carnegie Library opened in Dunfermline on August 29, 1883. Carnegie provided the site, building and furnishings for the library at a cost of about 8,000 pounds. The library building consisted of a library room, a gentlemen's reading room, a ladies' reading room, a recreation room, a smoking room, and a librarian's dwelling.

A painting entitled "The Dunfermline Demonstrations" by Andrew Blair and William Geddes records the day of the official opening of the library. It was commissioned by Andrew Carnegie and hangs in the Carnegie Birthplace Museum in Dunfermline. Andrew Carnegie and his mother, Margaret, accompanied by national and local dignitaries, arrived by carriage at the St. Margaret's Street entrance of the new library. In the painting, Margaret Carnegie is standing outside the carriage greeting townspeople. Two Town Councilors who had objected to the gift because it would increase rates (taxes) are standing with their backs to the demonstration.

From 1904 until 1922, the newly formed Carnegie Dunfermline Trust shared the management of the original library with the Town Council. In 1922, the Dunfermline Trust withdrew from the partnership, and the library became the responsibility of a Joint Committee of Town Councilors and householders of the Burgh. This occurred just after a new library extension was completed which doubled floor space, but did not dramatically alter the exterior of the original library. The recreation room and the librarian's quarters were removed.

Another extension to the Central Library opened March 2, 1993. The expanded four story facility houses a new children's library and audio department; a new local history library; new exhibition facilities at the upper level; and new book processing, branch, and external services operations areas at the basement level. Until 1996, this was the central library of the Dunfermline District Council serving a population of 130,000.

Interview Data

As a result of the reorganization of Local Government units, Fife Council was organized in April 1996. The population served in Fife Council is 307,000. The new unitary authority has absorbed the functions and geographical extent of four former authorities: Dunfermline District Council, Kirkcaldy District Council, North East Fife District Council and Fife Regional Council. The plan is for a decentralized, single tier system under one authority. The Dunfermline library is the largest in the whole system.

Currently, reorganization is the primary concern, and technology is secondary. The challenge is the integration of separate, incompatible operating systems. The four former authorities will be working together. A Libraries Review was in progress in the Summer 1997 for all of Fife Council. The charge of an information services working group was to determine the best solution for all of the libraries in the Fife Council. The four posts that have been recommended for the Fife Council are heads of each of the three areas (east, west, and central) and a systems librarian. Each of the area librarian positions also has a Fife-wide (strategic) responsibility. At this time, the objective is to get an upgrade to one system for all of the three districts in the Fife Council.

Both West Area (formerly Dunfermline District) and Central Area (formerly Kirkcaldy District) have automated systems for circulation and cataloguing. Central has the most up-to-date system (GENESIS). West's is older (DS). None of the systems in Fife is compatible. The Kirkcaldy

District is the only one of the three districts that has PCs or dumb terminals in all branches.

The East Area system was installed earlier. It has an in house cataloguing system, with an online catalogue for staff use only, and fiche/film and hard copy catalogues for the public. The North East Fife district does not have an automated circulation system. An automated systems working group that is investigating the feasibility of developing a common procedure for registration is in place. Funding has now been agreed upon for a unified, integrated, automated system for the whole of Fife Council Libraries (West, Central and East). Funding for technology is no longer likely to come from the book fund.

The largest amount (75%) of funding for the support of public libraries is from the central government, and the remaining amount (25%) is from the local government. Because of this, public library administrators must convince the central government of the need for funding, rather than putting the responsibility on local public officials. Local funding comes from Council rate (tax), and is topped by a government grant. The Carnegie Dunfermline Trust is supportive of the Dunfermline library. They make occasional gifts, which the library welcomes. These are small in scale and usually consist of a one-off donation of an item of equipment or a resource.

The budget cuts last year (1996) resulted in lower book funds, cuts in staffing, and the closing of branches. Projected cuts in staffing and branch closures did not occur this year. Government restructuring, although not in final mode in summer 1997, has resulted in the redeployment of staff. The chief librarian post, along with other vacant positions, has not been filled.

Pat Anderson was Acting Chief of Dunfermline District Libraries and West Area Libraries over the change over period from the former to the latter (1995-1996). She has now reverted to her former post (Lending Services Librarian) for West Fife Libraries. Anderson reported that the Dunfermline Central Library has had an automated circulation and cataloguing system for nearly twenty years. The current system is the second system, and is coming to the end of its lifetime. Dunfermline has a DS Module 3+ automated circulation control and cataloguing system. The integrated online staff only cataloguing system is not in MARC format. A microfiche catalogue is provided for the public and at the branches. The catalogue has subject, author, and title access, and is updated every two months. Checkout time is for three weeks, and fines are charged for overdue materials. The library lends CDs and tapes, but not videos. As of

December 1997, the library, including several branches, has an Internet connection.

There is a card catalogue for the local history collection in the Dunfermline library. The Carnegie Dunfermline Trust is funding the transfer of the Local History Department's catalogues and indexes (card) onto a computer database. A local company has been hired to key the holdings into the newly designed data base. There will be two public access terminals by summer 1998. Microfilmed historical documents and census records are available in the local history room. The census records are acquired when they become available. Microfilms of local newspapers are purchased from an agency of the National Library of Scotland.

The Carnegie Dunfermline Trust bought two CD-ROM computers, one for Central Library's Reference Department and one for the Children's Department. The Trust bought a microfiche index to old parish registers (OPRs) from before 1855. Old parish registers, on microfiche, are held in the Central Library. The original OPRs are held in the New Register House in Edinburgh. The local history department has purchased a *few* old cinema films. CD-ROMs for research purposes are available in the Reference Department.

Community input plays a large part in the selection and provision of library services. Counts are made of the total number of enquiries made. The total is broken down under topics. The counts are also conducted in small branches. When a new branch library was opened, a survey of the area to be served was conducted to determine what the customers wanted, including the hours the branch should be open. The library adjusted their services and collection to the wishes of the public.

Sally Joice, librarian for the lending library, discussed the stock ordering process in the Fife Council. She reported that books were provided for approval on a weekly basis. Various suppliers are used and a varying amount of processing is done by the supplier. The remainder of the processing is completed in-house by library staff.

In this financial year, professional branch staff are more involved in acquisitions. The responsibility for managing the budget is being given more to the people who are selecting and ordering the materials. Acquisitions librarians are given a sum of money which they can spend; however, there is currently no manual for collection development. A regular collection of books is available from a library supplier. Orders are placed as a result of the selections of the appropriate librarians. The library retains a key copy of each title. Suppliers provide the balance for the district. The library staff monitors the number of books in circulation.

Ordering is centralized within the West area (formerly Dunfermline

District). A matrix management system, away from hierarchial, is in place. There is local responsibility for subject areas, and the stock in a particular branch reflects the needs of that community. This demonstrates basic levels of service and fairness of service.

Joice noted that at one time there was a net book agreement with suppliers in which prices were fixed. This was cancelled, and now libraries can negotiate prices. Booksellers are bound by market supply and demand. Abandonment of the "Net Book Agreement"–price fixing by book suppliers and publishers–has led to increased levels of competition. Some suppliers have gone out of business.

Customers are charged 60 pence when they request a book. The cost for requesting material has practically doubled. As with the ongoing enquiry count, requests and suggestions are recorded. For adult users, computers with learning packages to support the open learning initiative are available.

When asked if censorship was a problem, each of the librarians responded basically in the same manner. They were protective of the right "not to censor." If materials were published in Great Britain, they were legal. As such, it was legal for the materials to be in the library. The primary concern mentioned was with children's access. Another librarian noted that it was illegal for a local authority, such as a library, to promote a homosexual lifestyle. This same librarian had been asked to find material in this area. The material is integrated with other material, and not shelved in a separate section.

Since the 17th November, Fife Council Libraries have a management team in place. This consists of a Libraries Policy and Learning Services Co-ordinator, Libraries Systems and Support Officer, Libraries Information Services Officer, and Libraries Cultural Services Officer. Each of these, with the exception of Systems and Support, also has a management role in one of the three areas. They are delegated to re-structure the staff at lower levels and to agree on revised methods of book supply and the like across the whole of Fife Libraries. This process is just beginning.

CITY OF YORK LIBRARIES

Background

The York library building, partly financed by the Carnegie United Kingdom Trust, opened in 1927. The library was built to fit into the scheme of the architecture of Museum Street, thus putting it on the same level as the other archives to human culture in the ancient city. Unlike the Croydon library system whose patrons are so ethnically diverse they need a commission on ethnic minorities, the York library system serves only a one percent non-Caucasian population.[23] The total population served is over 170,000.

As a result of the Unitary Authority changes, the North Yorkshire County Libraries–of which the North York Group library on Museum Street in York was a member–were divided into two systems: the City of York Libraries and the North Yorkshire County Library System. The North Yorkshire County Library system, headquartered in Northallerton, was one of the largest county systems in England. In the restructuring process, the city library, along with satellite villages, separated from the county system. The City of York Library is one arm of the Leisure Services Department. Each Department director reports directly to an elected committee. The decision-making body is comprised of the city counselors who are responsive to the advice of chief library officers.

Interview Data

According to Ellen Hamblett, stock librarian, "the City Council has made a conscious decision to become a flagship authority." Public libraries in the UK are administered by local authorities whose funding derives from local taxation, business rates and grants from central government. She also stated that currently the library receives no funds from the Carnegie United Kingdom Trust.

The library has a centralized acquisitions process. All branches have input, and customers are encouraged to contribute suggestions. Surveys are conducted on library use and a community survey on non-use was being planned at the time of the interview. The librarians use data from the surveys to guide collection development. For example, the Central library is currently in the process of stock refreshing in the areas of travel and the 300's (social sciences). The issue system is on-line and catalogue data are updated overnight.

The library has had computer cataloguing and issue system for a number of years. The present system is the third computer system, Genesis-SBS (Specialist Business Systems). It was developed out of Bookshelf, and is an amalgam of systems used in public and academic libraries. The Genesis system is being expanded to all seventeen branches; the only sites not yet connected are the smallest service points, the mobile library and the prison service. Genesis is a global system that displays what is in stock and where it is located.

Purchasing is done through library suppliers. Purchasing is also done through the suppliers using information received at regular book meetings.

Library suppliers can provide data in various formats to help book selection and ordering. The librarians keep a stock diary of collection areas so that they are aware of needs when they go to a warehouse to purchase books. The materials come to the library with library stationery, which includes a date label and a bar code. Adult fiction can be out on the shelf within one week to ten days of publication. The York Library does not buy MARC records catalogued by the British Library; instead, the library has an original cataloguer. The Dewey Catalogue System is the classification system used and cataloguing is to AACR II standards.

There is a restriction that the library cannot put fiction on the shelf until the material is published, but the library may have the fiction up to one month before the stores have it. If there is any cataloguing backlog, it is in nonfiction. Nonfiction is on the shelf in a six to eight week cycle because it is not bought in advance as often as fiction. When it comes to cataloguing, nonfiction requires more input to create the catalogue record.

There is an Online Catalogue for cataloguing and accessioning. There is no public access catalogue, but one is in development and should be up by the end of 1998. The system will begin on-line access at the largest service points and work towards the smaller service points.

Currently, to locate materials for customers, the staff member checks the computer at the reader's enquiry desk or the partial card catalogue in the reference department. The check-out process at the issue desk is electronic: the customer presents his/her reader card with a scanable barcode and the barcode is read off the book.

For patron electronic access, there are computers that run CD-ROMs in the reference department; however, there are no PCs for customers' personal use anywhere in the library. Internet access is in the experimental stage. The library has only had access for three or four months. There is one connected terminal which has the usual software blockers. As of December 1997, two other branches had the Internet.

Regarding censorship, Hamblett said that if material is published, it is considered available for the library to stock. Material cannot be obscene because it has passed inspection to be published. Lack of funds can mean certain items will not be bought or borrowed but, as over 70,000 books are published, no local government authority would be able to buy all items. All items published would be considered for stock but it is part of her job to ensure funds are not wasted and are used to their full potential. A certain amount of money is provided and library staff must decide what portion will be allocated to the upkeep of the collection. Appropriate allocation of funding for materials and for technology to facilitate access to those materials is an ongoing issue in all of the libraries.

CONCLUSIONS

The relationship of the growth and implementation of technology to the development and accessibility of library resources was the focus of this study. The data were collected by a combination of personal interviews, observation, and use of secondary resources.

Commonalities in all of the libraries studied were the commitment to service and the high level of professionalism of library managers and staff. It was evident that the library staffs were proud of their libraries as were the citizens who used the various resources and services. The Dunfermline Central Library (headquarters of the West Area Council), as a part of the Fife Regional Council, and the York City Libraries were being affected by local government reorganization. The Croydon libraries were not. In York, the city libraries had withdrawn from a large counties system, and conversely the Dunfermline Central library became part of a larger unitary authority.

In summary, Croydon Central Library had a stand alone accounting and acquisitions system. The library was using the GEAC cataloguing system and the ALSI accounting and acquisitions system. There was a public access catalogue showing the location of the copies and whether they were available. Public Internet access was available at several terminals.

Dunfermline Central Library, as well as the rest of the West Area Council, had the DS Module 3+ automated circulation control and cataloguing system with the online catalogue for staff use only. A microfiche catalogue was available for the public and at the branches. In December of 1997, it was reported that Internet access was available in the Central library and several branches.

York City Library had Genesis-Specialist Business Systems (SBS) catalogue online for cataloguing and accessioning for staff. There was no public catalogue but the library will have one by the end of 1998. Internet access was not available from York City Libraries at the time of the researcher's visit; however, as of December 1997, Internet access was available at the main library and two other branches.

Community and user involvement were solicited in each of the libraries through annual user surveys and enquiries counts. The data from these surveys were reviewed by committees and changes were implemented as resources became available.

Censorship is perceived as less of a concern in Great Britain than in the United States. Librarians agreed that materials that were published in the UK were legal and as such should be available for library customers. Due to limited funding, censorship becomes more of an economic issue than a social one.

In the words of Chris Batt, Borough Libraries and Museums Officer in

Croydon, information technology "cannot replace motivated staff, it cannot cover up bad management, it certainly cannot work without a clear vision of how services should progress into the future."[24] In each of the libraries in Great Britain visited in the summer 1997, staffs were motivated, high quality management was evident, and the vision for the future seemed to be reasonable and positive.

REFERENCES

1. Jaramillo, George R. "Computer Technology and Its Impact on Collection Development," *Collection Management*, Vol. 10(1/2), The Haworth Press, Inc., 1988, 3.

2. Ibid., 9.

3. Ibid., 9.

4. Ibid., 10.

5. Mary E. Jackson, "The Use of Technology in Public Libraries: A Brief Survey," *Public Library Quarterly* (1994) 14(2/3): 40.

6. Ibid., 46.

7. Chris Batt. *Information Technology in Public Libraries* (London: Library Association Publishing 1994), i.

8. Ibid., 2.

9. Ibid., 122.

10. Ibid., 19.

11. Ibid., 3.

12. Ibid., 9.

13. Ibid., 12-13.

14. Ibid., ii.

15. Ibid., iii.

16. Ibid., iii.

17. "Broad Brief for Croydon Suppliers," *Library Association Record Trade Supp.* December 1993, 9.

18. "Royal walkabout will allow Queen to meet shoppers in North End," *Croydon Advertiser.* 2 February 1996, 2.

19. *Croydon Advertiser.* 13 August 1997, 62.

20. "Cyberspace in a Victorian Setting," *News.* 28 February 1997, 13.

21. Customer Charter Croydon. *Libraries Museum & Arts*, flyer.

22. Chris Batt. *Information Technology in Public Libraries* (London: Library Association Publishing 1994), 15.

23. *City of York 1981-1991 Analysis: 100% Statistics.*

24. Chris Batt. *Information Technology in Public Libraries* (London: Library Association Publishing 1994), iii.

Making the Internet
a Part of the Library's Collection

Patricia H. Guarino

SUMMARY. Successfully implementing Internet access for the public's use in a public library requires careful planning and a commitment of both staff and financial resources. It also requires a new look at materials access and selection policies and procedures and the library's collection development process. Public libraries offering Internet access should have an Acceptable Use Policy (AUP) and specific procedures for patrons' use of the Internet service. The use of the Internet should be integrated into the library's collection development process and into the library's day-to-day operations. *[Article copies available for a fee from The Haworth Document Delivery Service: 1-800-342-9678. E-mail address: getinfo@haworthpressinc.com]*

INTRODUCTION

Providing access to the Internet in public libraries presents many new challenges to public librarians. Successful implementation of Internet access in public libraries requires careful planning and a commitment of both staff and financial resources. The project begins with planning for the actual physical communication connections and technical aspects of accessing the Internet and does not end until the public is empowered to efficiently use the information resources and tools available via the Inter-

Patricia H. Guarino is Systems Specialist at Hoover Public Library, 200 Municipal Drive, Hoover, AL 35216.

[Haworth co-indexing entry note]: "Making the Internet a Part of the Library's Collection." Guarino, Patricia H. Co-published simultaneously in *The Acquisitions Librarian* (The Haworth Press, Inc.) No. 20, 1998, pp. 91-100; and: *Public Library Collection Development in the Information Age* (ed: Annabel K. Stephens) The Haworth Press, Inc., 1998, pp. 91-100. Single or multiple copies of this article are available for a fee from The Haworth Document Delivery Service [1-800-342-9678, 9:00 a.m. - 5:00 p.m. (EST). E-mail address: getinfo@haworthpressinc.com].

net. The importance of planning and managing the physical network connections and providing for staff training are the critical first steps for a successful project implementation. However, this article focuses on the impact providing the public Internet access has on the library's policies and procedures and its collection development process.

IMPACT ON POLICY AND PROCEDURES

As soon as the decision is made to provide public access to the Internet, the current materials access and materials selection policies and procedures should be reviewed. According to Rosanne Cordell and Nancy Wootton, " . . . the Internet is far more than merely another format, such as libraries dealt with when deciding to collect videos or CDs; the Internet is a new publishing format, communication tool, repository of information, and art form" (7). A new look and approach to materials access and selection policies and procedures is required when providing Internet access.

A number of issues need to be considered to ensure that the library is proactive in determining how providing this new resource will impact its operations. Public libraries offering Internet access should have an Acceptable Use Policy (AUP) before providing access. Additionally, specific documentation should be provided detailing any rules and procedures that the patron is expected to follow when accessing the Internet from the library.

Acceptable Use Policy for Internet Access

A good way to begin the policy and procedure review is to examine other public libraries' Internet access policies and procedures. Although public libraries differ due to the varied clientele they serve, other libraries serving similar size populations and with similar community demographics provide a good starting point in understanding the impacts of providing public Internet access. Many public libraries that provide Internet access service also maintain a presence on the World Wide Web, that is, they have their own web site. Libraries with their own web site generally provide access to their "Acceptable Use Policies" for electronic information, sometimes referred to as "Internet Use Policy and Guidelines" or "Internet Use Rules and Procedures." These Internet AUPs provide guidelines for what is considered acceptable use for the computers and networks to which the library is providing access (Cordell and Wootton, 12). Kansas City Public Library, Berkeley Public Library, Chatham-Effingham-Liberty

Regional Library, St. Joseph County Public Library, and Houston Public Library are a few examples of libraries that provide a copy of their "Acceptable Use Policies" online (Kansas, Berkeley, Chatham-Effingham-Liberty, St. Joseph, Houston, web pages). A library's Internet Use Policy and Guidelines should address the following subjects: the purpose of providing the service, the responsibilities of the users and safety issues, and choosing and evaluating information sources.

Outlining how providing Internet Access service is viewed as part of the library's missions provides patrons and staff an understanding of how this information resource helps fulfill the library's role in the community. The library should be able to communicate what is valuable about the Internet and what the library's role is in helping patrons take advantage of the Internet. Without a clear vision of how the library wants to utilize this new information resource and how the library thinks providing Internet access will benefit its patrons, the staff will soon become overwhelmed and frustrated. Communicating expectations and timelines and taking the project one step at a time, while keeping long-term goals in mind, will ease the staff's stress level. By clearly communicating the library's plan, the patrons will understand the direction and time-frame the library is taking in implementing this new service.

The library board and staff must decide whether they are going to provide access equally to all users, that is, not filter or censor any Internet information based on the patron's age or the content of the web site. There is information on the Internet, just like in printed and other formats, that would not be considered appropriate for children. However, unlike other library materials, which are selected by the library staff, the information on the Internet does not require any selection procedure before being accessible to the public. It is important, therefore, that the library clearly outline in its AUP that the parents or legal guardians should be responsible for determining what resources are appropriate for their children, and if necessary, the parent should monitor their child's Internet sessions. There are tools, such as software programs, that can be used to "filter" or censor the information from the Internet. However, at this point in time, these software solutions are not one hundred percent dependable. Even with better designed and controlled software, many in the library profession believe that this issue should not be resolved with a software solution and that parents should be involved in their children's activities and any restriction of a child's access to the Internet is ultimately the parent or guardian's responsibility (Bern, 256-7). Each library should decide how best to handle this issue, keeping in mind the community served, and clearly communicating this decision in their policies.

When providing Internet access, it is important to educate children and youth about appropriate behavior on-line to ensure their safety. Children should be educated on the importance of not providing personal information, such as names, addresses, telephone numbers; how to handle information that makes them uncomfortable or that they feel is harmful to them; the importance of discussing with their parents their rules for using the online; and the dangers of agreeing to meet in person someone they have communicated with online. The National Center for Missing and Exploited Children produces a pamphlet titled "Child Safety on the Information Highway" that contains practical suggestions concerning online safety issues (Bern, 257). While the library can, through patron education and policy, highlight the responsibilities of the user and safety issues and concerns, the ultimate responsibility and enforceability remains with the patron and in the case of children, the parent and guardian.

Because the information accessible from the Internet is vast in not only the scope of the content and presentation, but also in the quality of the content and presentation, the Internet user must be responsible for being a good information consumer. The library board, staff, and patrons must realize that information on the Internet has not been subjected to the same selection policies which other information resources provided by the library have undergone. "Internet access challenges libraries' intellectual freedom policies because of its uncontrolled nature; no review or selection process within the library controls the files your patrons access" (Cordell and Wootton, 11).

The diversity and fluidity of the information on the Internet present the information consumer, the library patron, a challenge in determining the accuracy, completeness, and currency of the information (Houston Public Library, web page). While patrons have always been responsible for the final determination of the value of an information resource, other resources found in the library have been subjected to the library's stated collection development and materials selection policies. Because the information a patron retrieves from the Internet does not flow through this review process, more responsibility is put on the patron to question the validity of the resource. Although the library cannot be responsible for this evaluation and selection process, the library can provide printed and online job aids and training that educate the patrons on how to evaluate web information resources.

While it is important to address the issues outlined above in the library's AUP, if a copy of the AUP is provided online by the library, policy regarding copyright and misuse of technical resources should also be included. Additionally, the library needs to review its library card applications to ensure that they include a statement regarding electronic services, especially pertaining to electronic services provided to children.

Rules and Procedures for Accessing the Internet

Each library must determine its rules and procedures for accessing the Internet. Just as every library has developed specific procedures to meet its community's needs, the procedures for providing access to the Internet will be unique for each library. Again, a good starting point for determining the library's rules is to review existing rules and procedures from other libraries currently providing Internet access and to utilize the listservs that discuss public library issues. Based on a review of current public libraries' Internet access rules and procedures (Berkeley, Chatham-Effingham-Liberty, Houston, Kansas City, St. Joseph, web page) areas which a library must decide how it will handle are sign-up procedures, time limits, group use, printing and downloading rights, range of Internet services offered, use of user software, and extent of library staff support. A checklist should be developed asking specific questions in each of these areas and based on the staff's responses, specific procedures for the library can easily be developed.

A library's Internet rules and procedures will depend on the library's resources: hardware/software, staff, and financial. Each library must determine the best way to meet its patrons' needs according to its resource limitations. If a library has limited funds for hardware, then the computers that provide access to the Internet could also be used for other electronic information resources, such as CD-ROMS and on-line catalogs. Having the staff perform the Internet searching in some libraries might be the most productive use of resources (Cordell and Wootton, 9). An alternative to providing staff support for Internet searching is to provide introductory Internet classes for new users. Developing manageable Internet use procedures and rules is just as important for a successful project as having a dependable communication link and providing adequate staff and patron training. The rules and procedures also play a critical role in the community's perception of the value of this new information resource.

COLLECTION DEVELOPMENT–
INTERNET RESOURCES INTEGRATION

The planned integration of Internet resources into a library's collection development plans and day-to-day operations is often overlooked, which results in the failure of the library staff and patrons to fully utilize the

Internet as an information resource tool. It would be easy if the library could approach the Internet as just another format, like print, video, audio, CD-ROM, for providing patrons information. However, due to the nature of information available over the Internet, a more complex and time-consuming approach must be taken. This approach involves additional technical training for the staff, teaching the staff how to find, evaluate, and use Internet resources, and a determination of how and when it is appropriate to use the Internet to answer patrons' questions.

Technical Training

Comprehensive, customized training programs, which many times require extensive planning and preparation time, are necessary for librarians to become educated on accessing information on the Internet. Because of the complexity of the Internet, Internet training should be approached in multiple sessions with each training session addressing one of the Internet tools available at the library. Trainers can utilize existing general Internet training resources, and then customize the training materials to their specific training needs to achieve the most successful training programs. Library management must strongly support initial Internet training and on-going Internet training if they want their staff to integrate the Internet tools into their everyday work.

Librarians need to be trained not only on the basics concerning the different Internet services, but they also need training on how to use the search indexes and search engines available on the Internet. Many web sites on the Internet require understanding how the web site and usually some database is organized and accessed in order to efficiently use the information. Specialized training sessions on specific web resources may be required before the staff will feel comfortable using the information to meet a patron's need. One option for providing additional training on search engines and specific sites is to provide a monthly or quarterly list of reference questions to the staff to sharpen their Internet research skills. These training exercises could be completed over a period of two to four weeks and the results then shared with all the staff to extend the learning experience. This teaching method is especially suitable for reaching a library's part-time employees and provides flexibility to all employees because the training can be done at their own pace and as time permits during their regular work schedule.

Evaluating Internet Resources

As Daniel Ring stated in "The LIBRARIAN as a *Bookman*," ". . . it is important to know about Internet resources in the same way we know about a reference book" (62). When implementing Internet access within a library, the staff usually maintains a list of links, via a web page or bookmarks, that they use in their day-to-day operations. Before a library begins to use a web site to provide information to patrons, the web site should be reviewed and the same evaluation criteria (scope, authority, format, audience, cost) that are applied to other materials in its collection should be applied to the Internet resources.

When considering the scope of a web site, a librarian should not only consider the information provided by the site, but also, how the information from the site complements other web sites and other resources in different formats in the library's collection. Each site recommended by the library should add distinctive value to the total library collection.

When considering the format of the web site, the site's presentation of the information on the Web should be reviewed. Points to consider are whether the site's content is presented in a clear, understandable manner, how easily a patron can navigate around the site, whether the web site is overloaded with unnecessary graphics, whether the web site is designed to be viewed by a variety of web browsers, and whether additional training or patron resource aids would be required to successfully use the information.

Determining the authority of a web site is critical in the evaluation process. One of the strengths of the Web is the ease of publication and distribution of information to the world; however, this strength places a burden on the information consumer to determine the source of the information on a web site. A web site should not be used without first considering the source of the information because the timeliness and accuracy of data can be greatly affected by the authority behind the web site.

The web sites in the library's collection should be selected with the library's community of users in mind. Consideration should be given to not just the library's community, but the specific subset of users for a particular library's web page or department's bookmark file. For example, if developing links for the children's department web page or bookmarks, then only links to sites appropriate for children should be added.

Whenever possible, sites that have no fees associated with their provision of information or services should be considered over fee-based sites if the quality of the information/services is equal. Considering the information needs of the user and evaluating the cost of meeting those needs is still necessary in the online Internet information medium. Internet resources that require registration and fees should be reviewed and compared to other printed and electronic resources before a format selection decision is made.

Evaluating Internet web sites is a time-consuming process. Librarians have to learn to use reviews from computer and Internet magazines and on-line reviews to facilitate the review process. Librarians need to become connected to discussion groups and web sites that provide current information on new web sites and new Internet developments. The Scout Report, an electronic service provided by InterNIC's Net Scout Services, is a weekly Friday publication which provides reviews of valuable resources on the Web. The Scout Report is available at the Scout Report web site, http://www.scout.cs.wisc.edu/scout/report/, and through a mailing list. The TourBus, found at http://www.tourbus.com, is another web site that provides entertaining reviews on informative, useful, and sometimes just fun web sites twice a week. The TourBus can also be enjoyed through a mailing list. The Publib discussion list is an excellent source for Internet information, as well as other information of interest to public librarians. The Publib discussion list can be found at http://sunsite.berkeley.edu/Publib/, and the Publib archives can be easily searched. Instructions for subscribing to each of these listservs can be obtained at the web sites.

Integrating web resources into your library's collection is not a one-time process, but a continuous process that requires a commitment of on-going resources for selection and review, as well as maintenance functions to keep web site links current and to weed your on-line link collection. Web resources should not be viewed as replacements of current resources, but initially should be approached as a means to fill the information gaps in the library's collection and to supplement the library's collection by providing alternate access routes to information.

Appropriate Reference Use

The Internet is an excellent resource for certain types of information, such as, government information, current events and news, job and career information, community information, news groups and support groups, athletic event schedules, university information, and addresses/phone numbers. A lot of this information is not readily available in a reference book in a public library (Ring, 63). However, the Internet is by no means the solution to all patrons' questions. Learning when it is appropriate to use the Internet as an information resource is a skill that librarians will develop as they become more familiar with the strengths and weaknesses of the information on the Internet. Through reading reviews and various online and printed Internet publications, librarians can learn about the Web, but they will have to spend time online to feel comfortable and keep up-to-date with the resource. The vastness of this resource and the increasing depth of the information becoming available over the Web presents a formidable challenge to librarians.

CONCLUSION

In planning for the Internet access project, hardware, software, and staff requirements for implementing Internet access and for on-going provision of Internet access need to be considered. Ideally, the successful Internet access project results in the transparent use of Internet resources by the staff and patrons to meet their daily information needs. To reach this objective requires a dependable hardware and software configuration, well-trained staff, clearly defined Internet access policies and procedures, training tools and guidelines and rules that empower the patrons to fully capitalize on this new information resource, and a full integration of Internet resources into the library's collection development process and the staff's day-to-day operations.

The next step after successfully providing Internet access from the public library is to capitalize on the potential the Internet access provides to the libraries. Libraries which serve the community information resource role should be excited about using the communication power of the Internet to develop on-line community information resource centers. The possibilities are endless, such as, providing community based information services in health care, indexes to the local newspapers, subject guides to local magazine collections, monthly community events calendars, on-line vertical files indexes, searchable databases of unusual or typical reference questions, on-line reference and referral services, book and web site reviews, on-line bibliographies that link patrons to world-wide resources, full-text color children's books, job networks, and local school activities (McClure, 180-81, and Stearns, 55). With proper leadership and vision, public librarians are in a position to lead in the provision of value-added services via the Internet.

REFERENCES

Berkeley Public Library. "Berkeley Public Library Internet Use Policy." http://www.ci.berkeley.ca.us/bpl/files/usepolcy.html. (23 August 1997).

Berkeley Public Library. "BPL Internet Use Rules and Procedures." http://www.ci.berkeley.ca.us/bpl/files/bplrules.html. (23 August 1997).

Bern, Alan. "Access to the Internet in a Central Public Library Children's Room." *Journal of Youth Services in Libraries* 9.3 (1996): 253-62.

Chatham-Effingham-Liberty Regional Library. "CEL Regional Library Useful Web Sites–Disclaimer." http://www.co.chatham.ga.us/sites/disclaim.htm. (23 August 1997).

Cordell, Rosanne M. and Nancy A. Wootton. "Institutional Policy Issues for Providing Public Internet Access." *Reference Services Review.* 24.1 (1996): 7-12, 56.

Houston Public Library. "Houston Public Library Internet Use Policy and Guidelines." http://sparc.hpl.lib.tx.us/hpl/policy.html. (23 August 1997).

Kansas City Public Library. "Acceptable Use Policy Kansas City Public Library." http://www.kcpl.lib.mo.us/policies/aup.htm. (23 August 1997).

McClure, Charles R., William E. Moen, and Joe Ryan. *Libraries and the Internet/ NREN: Perspectives, Issues, and Challenges*. Westport, CT: Meckermedia Corp., 1994.

Ring, Daniel F. "The LIBRARIAN as a *Bookman*." *Public Libraries*. 25.1 (1996): 60-3.

St. Joseph County Public Library. "St. Joseph Public Library Computer Usage and Disclaimer." http://sjcpl.lib.in.us/homepage/Reference/ComputUsePolicy. html. (23 August 1997).

Sterns, Susan. "The Internet-Enabled Virtual Public Library." *Computers in Libraries*. 16.8 (1996): 54-7.

Cyberselection:
The Impact of the Internet
on Collection Development
in Public Libraries

Nancy Milnor

SUMMARY. Much attention has been given in the library literature to the controversy about the issue of restricting public access, especially that of children, to the Internet and some to the use of the Internet for reference and information delivery, but the impact of the Internet on materials selection has hardly been addressed. This article, which is based on interviews with working librarians, explores four ways in which use of the Internet is impacting selection in public libraries: selection tools and information, providing alternative sources of information, information access and currency and impact on materials budgets. *[Article copies available for a fee from The Haworth Document Delivery Service: 1-800-342-9678. E-mail address: getinfo@ haworthpressinc.com]*

Much attention has been given in the professional literature to the impact of the Internet on public libraries. The spotlight regarding the Internet has of course fallen on the controversy over kids' use of the medium and whether or not libraries ought to filter "obscene" material from it before serving it up to the public. A lot has also been written on the

---

Nancy L. Milnor can be contacted at 2310 Sealy, Galveston, TX 77550 (e-mail: nlmilnor@marlin.utmb.edu).

[Haworth co-indexing entry note]: "Cyberselection: The Impact of the Internet on Collection Development in Public Libraries." Milnor, Nancy. Co-published simultaneously in *The Acquisitions Librarian* (The Haworth Press, Inc.) No. 20, 1998, pp. 101-107; and: *Public Library Collection Development in the Information Age* (ed: Annabel K. Stephens) The Haworth Press, Inc., 1998, pp. 101-107. Single or multiple copies of this article are available for a fee from The Haworth Document Delivery Service [1-800-342-9678, 9:00 a.m. - 5:00 p.m. (EST). E-mail address: getinfo@haworthpressinc.com].

general topic of the need of public libraries to offer Internet access to the public and how this is best done. Some notice has been given as well to the use of the Internet for research and reference work, but the impact of the Internet on collection development has scarcely been addressed in the literature. Talking with librarians who do materials selection and use the Internet has turned up at least four ways in which the Internet impacts collection development.

SELECTION AIDS

Perhaps the most significant way in which the Internet is currently affecting collection development in public libraries is through its impact on the selection of materials. This occurs in several ways.

First is the use of selection tools, chief among which is the online bookstore Amazon.com (http://www.amazon.com). Elisabeth McMahon, Reference and Young Adult Librarian at the Rosenberg Library in Galveston, Texas, says that she often goes to this Web site rather than use *Books In Print* (BIP), which her library has on CD-ROM, as it is easier to access, has more information about the book, including a photograph of the cover, and, in addition, offers peer reviews as well as ones from the standard review media. "It is especially helpful," McMahon says, "to have reviews by other librarians or readers, as these people are in touch with what our patrons are likely to want and like." She went on to say that she imagines that it is especially important in this regard for small-budget libraries that cannot afford BIP online or a broad array of review media in paper format. Debbie Owen, a library director in Fairview Heights, Illinois, said with regard to the impact of these online bookstores, "I never use BIP any more and am thinking of dropping my subscription and just keeping *Forthcoming Books*." Barnes and Noble now has a Web site (http://www.barnesandnoble.com) that claims to have more titles than Amazon, and even independent bookstores are getting into the act. The Tattered Cover bookstore in Denver now has a Web site (http://www.tatteredcover.com) listing all of their titles.

Another helpful selection tool encountered on the Internet is bibliographies. There are sources in cyberspace for lists of "top" and "best" of current books, videos, etc., on various topics. McMahon says that the most useful and easily accessible of the lists are on Amazon.com. "These lists of recommended books are always up-to-date," says McMahon, "often up to the day you are looking at them, which makes them more valuable for current selection purposes than standard print bibliographies." She and others indicated that such lists are especially helpful when trying to select in a subject area with which one is not very familiar. Amazon.com also offers a feature wherein a user can leave her e-mail address attached to subject fields and she will be notified when important new titles in these subject fields are added to the Amazon.com inventory–in effect a virtual publication alert service.

In addition, Dana May, another reference librarian at the Rosenberg Library, pointed out that most publishers now have Web sites. Such sites help with getting bibliographic citations for new titles and allow the selector to browse the current and upcoming lists of publishers that regularly put out publications in areas in which one is looking for new materials.

Another way in which those interviewed indicated that the Internet aids in collection development is through belonging to listserves on which books and other materials are discussed by the participants. McMahon indicated that her young adult listserve (PUBYAC@NTSERNET.ORG) has been particularly helpful in selecting young adult materials. Eric Norton, reference librarian at Rosenberg Library, mentioned the usefulness of the award lists he has found on the Internet. He says there is a much more comprehensive database of book awards there (http://www.city-net.com/~lmann/awards) than can be found in any one print source and that he uses it a lot as a selection aid.

Barbara Kandt, Head of Adult Services at the Rosenberg Library, pointed out another important selection aid–Web sites such as Bibliofind (http://www.bibliofind.com) that help locate out-of-print (OP) books. Kandt thinks this Internet offering will be of special importance to libraries, as heretofore it has been extremely difficult for libraries to locate OP titles, as few could afford to pay the fees charged by OP search firms. These Web sites should help libraries to fill significant retrospective holes in their collections.

ALTERNATIVE INFORMATION SOURCES

Another way in which the Internet has great potential to affect collection development, though its impact is currently minor, is by providing alternative sources of information that will obviate the need to order a print or CD source. A good example in Texas at present is the *Encyclopedia Britannica*, the online version of which is being provided free to Texas public libraries by the State Library. Many large libraries will no doubt continue to purchase a print or CD version, but this online version has the potential to be a great materials budget saving force for smaller libraries, and, indeed, will provide the only version of this work for many really small and poor libraries that have never had the money to purchase Britannica. This situation is bound to be repeated in years to come with many other once costly sources of information. And as libraries are able to add increasingly more computer stations, enabling multiple users to simultaneously access online information, the need to buy paper copies of these sources will diminish.

A librarian in charge of ordering business-related materials at the Rosenberg Library said that he hoped that business directories would become available online and reduce the need for ordering print copies of these budget devourers. At least one publisher, however, Dun and Bradstreet, is charging more for the online than the print version of one of its major directories (*D&B Million Dollar Directory*). Upon being reminded of this fact, the business materials selector pointed out that clever librarians are finding sources for this type of information that are freely available, though not in the form of directories at one discreet site. Many major corporations, for instance, have Web sites, from which one can obtain all the sort of information that is contained in corporation directories and often additional information that the directories do not contain. Librarians thus could conceivably create their own directories from the Net. Another product mentioned that would no longer be ordered in CD is the PHONE-DISC, as apparently there is now a superior national phone directory available online called Switchboard (http://www.switchboard.com) that has 90 million phone listings. Adult Services Head Kandt said that the availability of this database free on line would allow her library to stop purchasing costly telephone directories.

Illinois Library Director Owen pointed out that for smaller libraries the limited number of Internet stations can be a significant drawback to replacing print sources with online ones. "I can get many more users to the info in a set of print encyclopedias than I can on electronic sources." She does admit though that it is an attractive prospect to drop some expensive print sources: "I have been thinking of dropping the *Thomas Register*, which is now online, except that [the] problem of having only two PCs pops up." The availability of sufficient equipment definitely goes into the print vs. online selection decision.

There has been prognostication for years that at some point periodicals and newspapers would be delivered to readers in electronic format rather than in print. Until recently getting online full text access to periodicals has proven prohibitively costly for all but the largest public libraries. However, increasingly, state libraries, regional libraries, library systems and other consortium-type entities are managing to strike good deals with the online periodical providers and are beginning to offer these databases free or at low cost to public libraries. This service is now being provided to public libraries in Texas by the State Library through *First Search*.

The online delivery of popular magazines and newspapers does not currently appear to be having a big effect on public library subscription lists, but with the advent of these databases available free online, Adult Services Head Kandt thinks public librarians will quickly begin to cancel print subscriptions to all their most esoteric titles and just keep getting the highly popular general periodicals, such as *Time* and *People*, in print format, until such time in the future when the public (which always lags behind librarians in expectations of technology) comes to prefer all their casual reading matter to be delivered in this manner. And, of course, once again the small, poor libraries have access for their patrons to a much greater range of periodical literature than they previously did.

Kandt also thinks the Internet is going to make a significant difference in the delivery of a type of material that public libraries are always in need of more of to meet the public's demand but can rarely afford in sufficient quantities–genealogy. If public librarians could have anticipated any one group making good use of the Internet, they might have guessed it would be genealogists, as these researchers are relentless in their quest for new sources of information and means to exchange the information they have garnered from their research. The appearance on the Internet of an ever-increasing number of genealogy Web sites should provide a much broader range of genealogical information to all public libraries and obviate the need to continue to purchase costly print materials in this subject area.

INFORMATION ACCESS AND CURRENCY

Librarians use the Internet to keep informed on subjects of interest to them as well as to seek out information on book titles available in specific subjects. I think this is a way in which librarians are using the Net that may eventually have the most profound effect on collection development. To begin, librarians use the Internet in a significantly different way than other people. Librarians have always approached the seeking out of information in an organized, logical, analytical manner; and they do this no differently on the Internet than with print sources. Librarians who use the Internet for reference purposes often do not have time to "surf"–they must go for the shortest route to the information they need, so that they can respond to the patron's information request as quickly as possible.

Librarians use the Internet in the same way to find information for themselves. There is a vast quantity of information available in cyberspace, and librarians, because of their approach, will get to a lot more of it that is pertinent than will other people. Almost every librarian I talked to who is involved with working with the public already has a great number of information sources "bookmarked" and continually bookmarks new Web sites. Librarians will come to use the information sources on the Internet to make themselves better informed in general, and this usage of the medium will affect their expertise and effectiveness in providing collections of materials to their patrons.

IMPACT OF TECHNOLOGY COSTS ON MATERIALS BUDGETS

Another way in which the Internet and other electronic information products have affected collection development is the impact that providing for the costs of technology has had on materials budgets. At this writer's institution and at those of others interviewed for this article, materials budgets have been reduced over the past decade to compensate for the cost of bringing in new technology and upgrading the old. The pace at which technology has changed in the current decade and at which it continues to change means that computer hardware becomes obsolete in only a few years and software in an even shorter time span. It has become a tremendous financial burden to keep up with replacement of the hardware and software to deliver electronic information products.

This revolution came at a time when public libraries were seeing their standard revenue sources (taxes) diminished because of hard economic times in their cities and counties or taxpayer revolt. And no new sources of local money have come along in most places to provide for the cost of technology. Large urban libraries have for the most part been able to manipulate their budgets, get tax increases, or secure corporate underwriters to cover the costs of technology. However, it is the small, rural libraries whose patrons could profit most from the information available on the Internet, as this medium has the potential to bring tons of information flooding into these libraries that their patrons never dreamed of having access to before. Unfortunately these libraries are the ones that have the hardest time getting the money to obtain technology. In the county in which this writer works, four of the eight public libraries have no Internet access, and this is in an area considered urban and fairly sophisticated. Fortunately the State Library of Texas is beginning to address this problem with grant programs, and the journal literature reveals that in other states also state libraries are beginning to work on the problem of funding technology for libraries of all sizes and locations.

And this summer brought the promise of a brave new world in the area of funding of technology for libraries with the announcement of the establishment of the Gates Library Foundation by Bill and Melinda Gates (see *American Libraries*, August, 1997, pp. 14-15). The Gates have invested $400 million in the Gates Library Foundation, and have indicated that they expect it to reach out directly to 8,000 libraries in the United States. Details about how the Gates Library Foundation will dole out the money to libraries across the land were expected to be released in the fall of 1997.

At any rate, the time has come when the costs of computer hardware and software need to be considered as part of libraries' materials budgets rather than as a peripheral, almost "toy like," category of purchase. Computer stations are now necessary to the delivery of much information and thus are legitimate costs of providing the public with the materials and information that were once supplied only in print format.

As the printing press profoundly affected people's access to information five centuries ago, the Internet is now so impacting people's access to information. It is inevitable then that the Internet will have a significant effect upon libraries and the way in which they get, store and deliver information to their users. This article has explored the ways in which the effect of this medium is being felt in the wee dawning seconds of this era. Doubtless the Internet will have an impact even the foreshadowing of which is not yet being perceived.

Selection and Evaluation
of Networked Information Resources

S. K. Hastings

SUMMARY. Public libraries need comprehensive, standardized evaluation strategies for the selection of electronic resources. This paper looks at networked information resources and discusses how to choose appropriate methods for selection. The role of traditional collection development criteria is expanded to include considerations that may be unique to electronic resources. In addition to the selection process, the measurement of how well a collection meets the information needs of users must be addressed. The second part of the paper discusses the different tools available to evaluate the use and effectiveness of a collection of networked electronic resources. *[Article copies available for a fee from The Haworth Document Delivery Service: 1-800-342-9678. E-mail address: getinfo@haworthpressinc.com]*

Public libraries are adding electronic resources as permanent components of the collection. Often these electronic resources replace existing print publications or augment the existing collection in some way. Electronic resources range from CD-ROM products, which may or may not be networked, to resources found on the Internet and the Web. This paper looks at networked information resources and discusses how to choose appropriate methods for selecting and evaluating these resources in a public library setting. For the purposes of this paper, networked information resources include all electronic information provided by the library

S. K. Hastings is affiliated with the University of North Texas School of Library and Information Sciences, POB 311068, Denton, TX 76203-1068.

[Haworth co-indexing entry note]: "Selection and Evaluation of Networked Information Resources." Hastings, S. K. Co-published simultaneously in *The Acquisitions Librarian* (The Haworth Press, Inc.) No. 20, 1998, pp. 109-122; and: *Public Library Collection Development in the Information Age* (ed: Annabel K. Stephens) The Haworth Press, Inc., 1998, pp. 109-122. Single or multiple copies of this article are available for a fee from The Haworth Document Delivery Service [1-800-342-9678, 9:00 a.m. - 5:00 p.m. (EST). E-mail address: getinfo@haworthpressinc.com].

109

over a network. The information can be provided at different levels of content and access and range from in-house networked CD-ROM products to selected Internet resources included on a library's Web site.

The evaluation of networked information resources fits into a larger evaluation scenario that looks at the quality of network services provided by a library. Bertot, McClure and Zweizig[1] include the following components of networked services: Technical Infrastructure, Content, Services, Support, and Management. Content is defined as "the information resources available on the network."[2] It is the selection and evaluation of network content that is addressed here.

Traditionally, collection development includes evaluation as an integral part of the selection process and in the measurement of how well a collection meets the information needs of users. Many of the same selection criteria used for print resources apply to electronic resources but some important additional criteria should be used to evaluate networked electronic resources. The first part of the paper looks at selection criteria and evaluation of resources. The second part of the paper discusses the different tools available to evaluate the use and effectiveness of a collection of networked electronic resources.

SELECTION CRITERIA

Librarians evaluate networked information resources to decide whether an information source should be linked to a resource guide or library Web site, added to the library's collection, or to use the information to meet the information need or query of a specific user. The problem of sifting through a mass of advertising material and vanity publications on the Internet in order to find quality information is a complicated and time-consuming process.[3] Matthew Ciolek[4] expresses a concern that the WWW (World Wide Web) may become the MMM (Multi-Media Mediocrity). The concern regarding mediocrity focuses even more importance on the evaluation of electronic resources.

James Rettig notes that many Internet sites that select and review Internet information resources rely on subjective values of style and "coolness," instead of focusing on information content. The development of subject resource guides or bibliographies is a logical role for librarians, extending to the electronic environment the traditional librarian's role of evaluating, selecting, and organizing published information.[5] In order to assure our users that they can trust our evaluation, we need to standardize the criteria we use when selecting electronic resources to add to our collections.

The evaluation of print reference sources enjoys a substantial literature. Katz[6] as well as Bopp and Smith[7] devote entire sections of their textbooks on reference work to "Evaluating Reference Sources," and list authority, scope, purpose, audience, format, and cost as primary selection criteria. With the growth of concern about quality of networked information, an increased number of publications in the print literature and on the Internet address the issue of criteria for evaluating Internet information resources.[8-17]

While criteria for the selection of print materials may be applied to networked resources, additional criteria are needed in the evaluation process. The following discussion of authority, scope, content, design and format, purpose and audience, ease of use, and cost as they apply to networked resources presents some of the questions we need to ask. The discussion includes information from many sources and subjective observation. Specific references are given for unique contributions or "new" terminology.

Authority

Traditionally published, print materials are filtered in three ways. First, if it is written by an authoritative source such as the federal government, it is usually accepted at face value as having validity. Second, if a publisher authenticates it as part of an editorial or peer review process, it is generally accepted as reliable. Third, if librarians as part of collection development evaluate it, it is generally accepted as authoritative. As part of the collection development process, librarians expend a lot of energy verifying the validity and authenticity of materials through reviews and in-hand examination. Electronic resources do not have such formal filtering processes in place. In the process of print publishing a series of editorial checks reduce the appearance of low-quality information. These checks are mostly missing in the electronic publishing process.

With electronic resources, authority becomes a primary selection criterion. In print resources, information on authority and scope comes from the publishing process and may come from introductory notes. Kovacs et al.[8] note a tendency for Internet resources not to offer useful scope notes or contain information about the credentials of the producers. Tillman[9] considers one of the key indicators of quality to be the ease of identifying the scope and criteria for inclusion; she then decides whether these factors match her needs.

As in the print environment, an important resource for selection with electronic resources is the use of reviews. Unfortunately, as noted by Rettig,[10] consistent, authoritative reviews of Internet information resources are not yet widely available. Some publications, which have a tradition of reviewing print reference resources, have started reviewing Internet sites; one example is "WebWatch" in *Library Journal.* In addition, the Internet has seen a growth in the number of Web sites that select, review, or provide awards for Internet information resources. (A list of URLs and evaluative criteria is available from Alastair Smith as Appendix A to his excellent work on evaluation.)[11] Again, it is noted that the criteria for some of the prominent Web review sites are primarily subjective and based on the concept of "coolness" and overall effect, rather than information content.

While ratings including "coolness" and similar criteria contribute to the vitality of the Web, they tend to omit consideration of issues of content and authority with which librarians are more concerned.[12] Raters also tend to assume an absolute value for rating a site, while Rosenfeld,[13] in satirizing these services, makes the point that the value of a resource will vary for different audiences and in different subject domains.

On the other hand, there are sites, particularly those managed by librarians (like the Argus Clearinghouse), which tend to place more emphasis on content and authority when evaluating sites.[14]

Scope

What items are included in the electronic resource? Is the scope only implied, or is it stated through meta-information such as an introduction? Does the actual scope of the resource match expectations? When using scope as a criterion, the following aspects are important to include in the evaluation process:

- Breadth: What aspects of the subject are covered? Is the resource focused on a narrow area or does it include related topics?
- Depth: What is the level of detail provided about the subject? Also, see the discussion of audience level below.
- Time: What time periods are covered? Is the information in the resource limited to certain time periods?
- Format: A resource that provides links may restrict its scope to certain classes of resources. For example, Telnet, Gopher, or FTP (File Transfer Protocol) resources may be excluded from a Web site.

Content

When evaluating content it's important to make a distinction between sites that only provide links to other resources, and those that provide original information. This is similar to Katz's distinction between control-access-directional sources (e.g., bibliographies as well as indexing and abstracting services) and source-type works (like encyclopedias and fact-books). Both have their place, but Grassian[15] argues that a source should have an appropriate balance between inward-pointing links and outward-pointing links. Lists of resources that look promising, but turn out to simply contain more links, can frustrate users.

The format of the content becomes more critical in the electronic environment when specialized software and hardware are required to access information. Many authors (e.g., Caywood[16]) include a criterion of compatibility. This may include consideration of whether the site works with different versions of browsers or Lynx, or uses common and standardized multimedia formats.

There are several other factors related to the content criterion to be considered including the accuracy, authority, currency, and uniqueness of a resource.

- Accuracy: Is the information in the resource accurate? A resource may be checked against other resources or against information that the evaluator has. Is the information fact or opinion? Are there political, ideological, or other biases? The Web has become a prime marketing and advertising tool, and it is advisable to ask what motivation the author has for placing this information on the Net. As with other vanity information, too frequently the answer is that the information is placed to advertise, or to support, a particular point of view.
- Authority: Does the resource have some reputable organization or expert behind it? Is the author a respected authority? Are the sources of information stated? Is the information verifiable? Can the author be contacted for clarification or to be informed of new information?
- Currency: Currency, in theory, should be where Internet sources have an advantage over print sources. However, it can be difficult to determine the date of update of Internet resources. While many sites explicitly include a date of last revision, many do not. The noncommercial nature of some information on the Internet can make for less current sources. Stoker and Cooke[17] point out that Internet versions of common reference works are often the out-of-copyright older editions. How frequently do updates occur? Remember that the date stamping of files, determined by many browsers, indicates the date of change in the physical file but this may not reflect the currency of the information.

- Uniqueness: Is the content of the resource available in other forms (at other sites, in print, on CD-ROM)? What advantages does this particular resource have? If the resource is derived from another format, does it have all the features of the original? Have extra features been added? Does it complement another resource, for example, by providing updates to a printed source? On the Internet, a resource may be available from a number of different sources and in different editions and formats. When a particular site is not available when required, this redundancy can be a plus, but a process for noting editions should be used.

It's important to remember that the facets of the content criterion mentioned above also need to be applied to the links made to other resources. If the value of the site lies in its links to other resources, are the links kept up to date? Are the linked resources appropriate? Is it clear when an external site is being referred to?

The last of the content issues is not the least. Most of the information content on the Web is still text and the quality of writing remains essential for the content to be communicated clearly. Don't let the glory of hypertext linking and sexiness of the multimedia environment mislead you. Is the text well written?

Design and Format

Do the visual effects enhance the resource, distract from the content, or substitute for content? If audio, video, virtual reality modeling, or other effects are used, are they appropriate to the purpose of the source? One of the most important design criteria for electronic resources is navigational design, mentioned below in the context of browsability and organization.

Purpose and Audience

What is the purpose of the resource and is it clearly stated? Does the resource fit the stated purpose? Does the stated purpose fit the intended audience for the resource? Who are the intended users of this resource? What level of audience is the resource intended for: a subject expert, a layperson, or a student? Does the user group have the needed level of connectivity to access the resource and all of its features? Will the resource satisfy the needs of the intended users? (See part 2 below on measures of effectiveness for further discussion of meeting user needs.)

Ease of Use

Ease of use of networked information resources introduces new criteria for consideration. Is the resource convenient, and can it be used effectively? Gurn[18] introduces a criterion, "conviviality," for the ease with which a user interacts with a service. Caywood[19] makes connectivity a significant criterion, consider whether a site is frequently overloaded and whether the URL (Uniform Resource Locator) is stable. There are several other aspects of ease of use that need to be considered in the evaluation of networked information resources:

- User Friendliness: Is the resource easy to use? Are any necessary special commands clear? Is help information available? Is there a 'no-frames' option? Are menu design, readability of screens and other user interface issues considered?
- Computing Environment: Can the resource be accessed with standard equipment and software, or are special software, passwords, or network protocols required? To ensure that the resource will work with all connections and user interfaces, it is useful to test resources with a variety of browsers and connections. Keep in mind your users with visual impairments or Lynx only connections. Also, if the correct helper applications are not installed, images and other multimedia may create problems. Note that if users are in a contained computing environment such as an Intranet or on workstations in a particular library, this criterion is less important.
- Searching: How effectively can information be retrieved from the resource? Is a useful search engine provided? What operators and ranking features are available? Is use of the search engine interface intuitive? Does the search engine index the whole resource? Perhaps most important is the realization that searching is not evaluation. Search engines select, compile, and determine access points for retrieving information on the Web sites or pages. They do not evaluate content. For more on this, Tillman provides an excellent investigation of search engines and evaluation.[20]
- Browsability and Organization: Is the resource organized in a logical manner to facilitate the location of information? Is the organizational scheme appropriate for the resource (e.g., chronological for an historical source or geographical for a regional resource)?
- Interactivity: Where interactive features such as forms, Java scripts and CGI (Common Gateway Interface) scripts are provided, do they work? Do they add value to the site? What do you do with the information collected?

Cost

Cost is an important criterion used for evaluating print resources but it has been given less emphasis in considering networked resources due to the perception of the Internet as "free." However, costs exist and they are likely to become more important as selection criteria for electronic resources. Costs can be divided into costs of connecting to the resource and costs associated with the use of the intellectual property contained in the resource. Internet users paying traffic charges already have to consider the costs of connection, and they may want to include this in criteria for selection. For example, they may favor text-based rather than image-intensive sites, if the information content is the same.

Increasingly, there will be sites where a charge is made for the intellectual content of the site. Libraries have been dealing with pay-per-use online services such as Dialog for many years, but the Internet has created an opportunity to make services available to end users for a fee. Libraries have an important role in negotiating subscriptions and site licenses for organizational access to services that charge.

If online transactions are used to pay for information, the security of these transactions at a site may become important. Services that have a version that costs money may be available with limited functionality, for trial periods, or for free. Trial periods provide an opportunity for "testing" the resource before adding it to the collection.

Summary of Selection Criteria

In summary, there are basically two ways to look at evaluation. Objectively, you can assess the validity, reliability, and authenticity of information. On a more subjective level, you must determine whether given information is pertinent for your needs. Valid information issued by NASA may not be pertinent if you're looking for space travel trends in science fiction.[21] In addition to checking a Web page for its critical elements—the header, body, and footer—to determine the author and source, we need to consider using the Web or the network itself to collect data about the use of the resource. The question of whether or not the networked electronic resource meets the needs of our users must be asked. In the following section, evaluation methods for measuring effectiveness are presented.

MEASURES OF EFFECTIVENESS

Public libraries need a regular program of data collection, performance measures, and related statistics of networking activities and services.[22] In order to determine if a networked resource meets the information needs of your clientele, several methods or measures of effectiveness need to be employed. There is a growing body of literature beginning to address the need for cohesive evaluation methods that include both quantitative and qualitative data collection techniques. The resulting research reports include a focus on the user and how the user interacts with networked services.[23] Many of these user-centered approaches could work extremely well for the evaluation of networked resources in public libraries.

Evaluation methods can help libraries determine which networked information resources are effective as well as identify the costs required to maintain the resource. Bertot, McClure and Zweizig[24] suggest a number of ways to categorize evaluation measures for networked services. The categories that are directly useful for the evaluation of networked resources are summarized as:

- The number and types of people using the resource.
- Costs or resources required to provide the service or resource.
- The degree to which the resource meets the objectives of the library.
- Service quality as measured, for example, by the percentage of transactions where users acquire the information they need.
- Impact or degree to which using the resource empowers the user.
- Usefulness as the degree to which the resource is useful or appropriate for the individual user.

Moen and McClure[25] provide a description of quantitative and qualitative data collection techniques used in an assessment of the Government Information Locator Service (GILS). They include the use of site visits, focus groups, surveys, content analysis, transaction log analysis, scripted user assessment and policy review. A description of the techniques that may be appropriate for the evaluation of networked resources follows:

- User Surveys: survey instruments designed to assess the user's rating of the resource.
- Scripted User Assessment: a method for capturing user's ratings, similar to user surveys.
- Content Analysis: a procedure to analyze the content of the networked resource including aesthetics, readability, and relevancy judgment.
- Transaction Log Analysis: a method that provides data for analysis of user transaction activity at a Web site. See Rubin[26] for an overview of how to set up procedures to capture log files.

If we combine the above techniques and measures for effectiveness, we have the framework for an evaluation plan that includes quantitative and qualitative measures. Each of the techniques has strengths and weaknesses that are described below. It is important to note that ideally, evaluation is part of the strategic planning process in public libraries. It is very difficult to measure and evaluate after the fact. The evaluation of networked resources should be part of the initial planning process when a library adds electronic resources to the collection.

User Surveys

The library staff can use questionnaires to obtain information from a large number of individuals. Surveys may be delivered by mail or hand-delivered, person-to-person, by computer, or by telephone. Questionnaire surveys provide ease of analysis and summarizing data is fairly simple. It is possible to collect data from large numbers of people in short time periods. Surveys can be confidential and the process is relatively inexpensive. However, questionnaires that collect accurate data are not simple to design and administer. It's a good idea to test the survey with stakeholders and a sample from the target population before finalizing the instrument. Substantial planning time and expertise are required to collect accurate data. Return rates may be quite low and data are restricted by the questions that are asked.

Users can also be surveyed by observation and interview. These are more expensive and the data collected are more difficult to analyze. Observers must be skilled in the process of observation. The data collected by observation is filtered through individual perspective and values so it may not be as accurate. Individual interviews are time consuming and a skilled interviewer is needed to design effective questions and conduct a good interview. Group interviews or focus groups may also be used to collect information from small groups of people. A skilled facilitator should lead the group and another person is needed to record and document the comments and responses from the group. Focus groups are useful to stimulate thinking, to gather different views on the same subject, and to get consensus about a program or resource.

Scripted User Assessment

This is a technique that fits the electronic environment extremely well. Users can be asked to rate an electronic resource at the site while using the resource. Data are easy to collect and analyze and it is an inexpensive process once the script has been designed. Scripts may be interactive so that certain responses will lead to additional tasks for evaluation. The user can be led through the system or resource and asked for specific responses at each level. The questions can be both multiple choice and short answer, providing a rich data pool. Analysis of the data, although not difficult, can be time-consuming depending on the narratives collected.

Content Analysis

Content analysis is multi-faceted. It can include use of the data collected during the selection process of the resource as well as the data collected from interviews, focus groups, survey questionnaires and scripted online assessment. Quality and usability of the information resource are the focal points for this type of analysis.

Transaction Log Analysis

This technique is similar to using existing library records to provide quantifiable evidence of activities and results. Libraries currently use registration materials, financial records, usage counts, circulation statistics, etc., to evaluate resources and programs. Transaction log files measure the number of hits or accesses a Web site receives in a duration of time. Log analysis requires a software program to collect the data. The programs are free or inexpensive but the data need to be analyzed by an expert to isolate the variables. Rubin[27] gives the following examples of statistics that can be tracked by the access log:

- The percentage of users accessing the site from a specific domain (e.g., com, edu, net, gov).
- The number of hits the server gets during specific hours.
- The number of hits every page receives within a site.
- The path by which a user navigates through a site, also called threading, can tell you where the user entered a site, what page the user exits from, how much time the user spends on a page and how much time the user spends downloading a page.

Summary of Measures of Effectiveness

The process of creating and refining the assessment and evaluation tools that libraries can use to measure the effectiveness of networked resources has just begun. Assessment and evaluation should be the foundation for determining the selection of electronic resources added to a library's collection. There is no single method for evaluation of effectiveness. A suite of methods is needed and we need to standardize what that suite includes. The questions we need to keep asking are:

1. What is the scope of the library's electronic resources?
2. How much use do the resources receive and why are they used?
3. What types of users access the resources and what activities do they perform?
4. Do the users find what they need?
5. What are the costs for providing the resource?
6. How does access and use of the resource affect the user in terms of productivity, quality of life, and other traditional performance indicators?
7. What types of evaluation techniques are appropriate to measure effectiveness in the electronic environment?

CONCLUSIONS

The intent of this paper is to provide collection development staff in public libraries an overview of some of the methods and techniques available and useful in the selection and evaluation of networked information resources. In a larger context, the design and implementation of cohesive, standardized programs of evaluation of networked services are some of the most exciting challenges of our profession. The process begins when an electronic resource is added to the collection, continues with the maintenance of the resource and culminates when the resource meets the information needs of our users in the most efficient method available. Without evaluation we'll never know what "efficient" means.

REFERENCES

1. John C. Bertot, Charles R. McClure and Douglas L. Zweizig, *The 1996 National Survey of Public Libraries and the Internet: Progress and Issues. Final Report.* (Washington, DC: National Commission on Libraries and Information Science, 1996). See <URL:http://www.istweb.syr.edu/Project/Faculty/McClure-NSPL96/NSPL94_4. html>

2. Ibid, p. 5.

3. Alastair G. Smith, "Testing the Surf: Criteria for Evaluating Internet Information Resources." *The Public-Access Computer Systems Review* 8, no. 3 (1997). See <URL:http://www.vuw.ac.nz/~agsmith/evaln/index.htm>

4. T. Matthew Ciolek, "Today's WWW–Tomorrow's MMM? The Specter of Multi-Media Mediocrity," *Computer* 29 (January 1996): 106-108. See <URL:http://

computer.org/computer/co1996/r1toc.htm> under "Departments." Also see <URL: http://coombs.anu.edu.au/WWWVL-InfoQuality.html for online resources relevant for evaluation.

5. James Rettig, "Beyond 'Cool': Analog Models for Reviewing Digital Resources," *Online* 20 (September 1996): 52-54, 56, 58-62, 64. See <URL:http:// www.onlineinc.com/onlinemag/SeptOL/rettig9.html>.

6. William A. Katz, *Introduction to Reference Work* (New York: McGraw-Hill, 1992).

7. Richard E. Bopp and Linda C. Smith, *Reference and Information Services: An Introduction*, 2nd ed. (Englewood, CO: Libraries Unlimited, 1995).

8. Diane Kovacs, Barbara F. Schloman and Julie A. McDaniel, "A Model for Planning and Providing Reference Services Using Internet Resources," *Library Trends* 42 (Spring 1994): 644.

9. Hope N. Tillman, *Evaluating Quality on the Net* (Bedford, MA: The Internet Access Company, 18 May 1997). See <URL:http://www.tiac.net/users/hope/ findqual.html or http://www.infotoday.com/cil.html>

10. James Rettig, *Putting the Squeeze on the Information Firehose*: *The Need for 'Neteditors and 'Netreviewers* (Williamsburg, VA: College of William and Mary, 8 November 1995). See <URL:http://www.swem.wm.edu/firehose.html>.

11. Alastair G. Smith, "Testing the Surf: Criteria for Evaluating Internet Information Resources."

12. Ibid.

13. Louis B. Rosenfeld, "Web Architect: Get Rich Quick! Rate Web Sites!" *Web Review*, 26 April 1996. See <URL:http://www.webreview.com/96/04/26/ webarch/index.html>.

14. The Argus Clearinghouse. See <http://www.clearinghouse.net/chhome. html>.

15. Esther Grassian, *Thinking Critically about World Wide Web Resources* (Los Angeles, CA: University of California, Los Angeles, 20 February 1997). See <URL:http://www.library.ucla.edu/libraries/college/instruct/criti cal.htm>.

16. Carolyn Caywood, *Resources Library Selection Criteria for WWW* (Infi-Net, August 1997). See <URL:http://www6.pilot.infi.net/~carolyn/criteria.html>.

17. D. Stoker and C. Cooke, "Evaluation of Networked Information Sources." In *The Information Superhighway*: *The Role of Librarians, Information Scientists, and Intermediaries*. Edited by A.H. Helal and J.W. Weiss. (Essen: Publications of the Essen University Library, 1995).

18. Robert M Gurn, "Measuring Information Providers on the Internet," *Computers in Libraries* 15 (January 1995): 42.

19. Caywood, *Resources Library Selection Criteria for WWW Resources*.

20. Tillman, *Evaluating Quality on the Net*.

21. Gene Wilkinson, *Evaluating the Quality of Internet Information Sources* (Athens, GA: University of Georgia, 20 May 1997). See <URL:http://itech1.coe. uga.edu/faculty/gwilkinson/webeval.html>.

22. Bertot, McClure and Zweizig, *The 1996 National Survey of Public Libraries and the Internet*: *Progress and Issues. Final Report*.

23. See recent work by Charles R. McClure. <URL:http://istweb.syr.edu/Project/Faculty/McClure>.

24. Bertot, McClure and Zweizig, *The 1996 National Survey of Public Libraries and the Internet: Progress and Issues. Final Report.*

25. William E. Moen, Charles R. McClure, June Koelker and Erin Stewart. "Assessing the Government Information Locator Service (GILS): A Multi-Method Approach for Evaluating Network Services," Proceeding of 60th ASIS Annual Meeting: Washington, DC, November 1-6, 1997 (Medford, NJ: Information Today, Inc., 1997) 34: 67-77.

26. Jeffrey H. Rubin. "Log Analysis–A Brief Overview" (Syracuse, NY: Syracuse University, October 18, 1996). See URL:http://istweb.syr.edu/Project/Faculty/logs.html.

27. Ibid.

Collection Development of Electronic Resources at the Science, Industry and Business Library (SIBL)

Ellen H. Poisson

SUMMARY. Selection of electronic resources should be integrated into existing collection development policies and procedures. Such selection is complicated by the number of options available, such as: multiple formats and access methods; pricing schemes; interface designs; differences in scope, timeliness and coverage; and technical support issues. At SIBL, the selection of electronic resources was done by an interdepartmental committee which drew upon subject specialists and which based selection on the existing collection development policy. The implementation of electronic resources at SIBL was accomplished in tandem with training for staff and for the public. *[Article copies available for a fee from The Haworth Document Delivery Service: 1-800-342-9678. E-mail address: getinfo@haworthpressinc.com]*

INTRODUCTION

Electronic resources in public libraries can vastly expand the access to information by library users. Today, these electronic resources include not

Ellen H. Poisson was former Assistant Director for Electronic Resources, Science, Industry and Business Library, New York Public Library. Her current position is Associate Professor at the Pratt Institute of the School of Information and Library Science, 220 Willoughby Avenue, Brooklyn, NY 11205.

[Haworth co-indexing entry note]: "Collection Development of Electronic Resources at the Science, Industry and Business Library (SIBL)." Poisson, Ellen H. Co-published simultaneously in *The Acquisitions Librarian* (The Haworth Press, Inc.) No. 20, 1998, pp. 123-130; and: *Public Library Collection Development in the Information Age* (ed: Annabel K. Stephens) The Haworth Press, Inc., 1998, pp. 123-130. Single or multiple copies of this article are available for a fee from The Haworth Document Delivery Service [1-800-342-9678, 9:00 a.m. - 5:00 p.m. (EST). E-mail address: getinfo@ haworthpressinc.com].

only the traditional bibliographic databases, but also electronic encyclopedias, computer assisted instruction programs, and the Internet. By making carefully selected electronic products available to users, a public library can supplement its print collection and provide access to information not as easily obtained in traditional resources. A public library can also provide its constituency with an important learning experience and even training in the efficient use of electronic resources, including the Internet.

Electronic resources historically have not been implemented in public libraries at the same rate as in academic and special libraries, mostly because of the cost of the resources themselves, the technical expertise required, and because of challenges in training the public to use the resources. In the early days of online searching, learning and keeping up-to-date in the command languages required a considerable investment of time, and payment of connect-time charges and per-use royalties limited use of these systems by most public libraries.

Many of the electronic resources that are available today are easier to use and sometimes contain information that is not available or not as up-to-date in the printed resources. However, there are still multiple challenges in bringing electronic resources into the collection development plan of a public library. The actual selection process is becoming increasingly complex, and needs to be well integrated into the overall collection development process. The initial selection of electronic resources is only the beginning, because such resources require on-going updating and technical support, as well as training for library staff and patrons. Of the greatest importance is a system to monitor the levels of use of each product, so that future renewal and new selection decisions can take these data into account.

INTEGRATED COLLECTION DEVELOPMENT

Selection of electronic resources must first and foremost be integrated into the overall collection development plan.[1] A library's electronic resources need to have an integral relationship with the print collection. The starting point should be the collection development policy: in which subject areas would electronic resources strengthen the collection and provide improved access to information for a significant number of users? If the new electronic resources will provide references to articles but not to the full text, how will the increased demand for those materials be satisfied? If an electronic database is to be licensed or purchased, will a subscription to the printed counterpart be continued? What about other print or electronic resources in the same field? The full impact of the addition of new electronic resources needs to be considered carefully in terms of the present printed collection and patron needs, particularly since each electronic resource will usually absorb a significant proportion of the collection development budget, as well as personnel resources.

The integration of collection development of electronic resources into the on-going selection process may be done in a number of ways. Selection criteria for electronic resources should be included in the collection development policy. The procedures for selection decisions in each core subject area may be updated to include a periodic review of new or improved electronic products. In larger libraries, a team of librarians and technical resource people may be formed specifically to review electronic resource selections. It may also be that there is one budget for printed and electronic resources. If this is not so, both budgets should be reviewed by an oversight committee or by library management to be sure that they are kept in reasonable proportion to each other.

There is yet another reason for integration of electronic selection into the overall collection development process. Decisions made on electronic resources which replace or duplicate printed resources will affect the longer term retention policies for the printed resources. Is it critical that a certain index be retained in perpetuity and therefore should an archival printed copy be kept? Is the demand so high for this resource that a subscription to the printed material must be maintained in addition to the electronic license?

ELECTRONIC COLLECTION DEVELOPMENT

Collection development librarians in public libraries are faced today with increasing complexity in the options available for providing access to electronic resources. Only a few years ago the decisions were relatively simple: there was a choice of purchase of a printed index or online access via a commercial vendor on demand. In public libraries, such resources were usually not available to the public, but only searched by librarians for ready reference or for patrons for a fee.

With the advent of CD-ROM databases in 1986, the options became a bit more complicated because now there were three choices: a printed index, online access with pay-as-you-search charges, or a flat annual fee to purchase or license a database on CD-ROM. The flat fees which were available with CD-ROM licenses made possible direct patron access to electronic resources for the first time in libraries that needed to be able to predict precisely what acquisitions expenditures would be.

Today the selection of electronic resources has become even more complex because there is yet a fourth option in addition to the options outlined above: a number of vendors have begun to offer database access over the Internet as well as over traditional dial-up networks, on CD-ROM, and in printed versions. Internet access may also involve a flat fee or may be charged on a pay-as-you-go basis.

Selection decisions should include the following criteria:

- Does the collection development policy include this subject area as one that is appropriate for electronic resource collection? (If not, does the policy need to be updated?) What dates of coverage are desirable? What aspects of this subject are the most important to the library's users?
- Who will be using the resource? Will it be used by library staff for their own work and education? Will it be searched by reference librarians as needed for the public? Will the resource be available for searching by the public? Must the interface be highly user-friendly?
- How much money is available for this resource? Must there be a flat-fee or could a pay-as-you-go scheme be considered? Are there opportunities for consortium pricing or negotiation with the vendor?
- Is networking an option or must the resource be made available on a stand-alone system? Is it possible and is there likely to be a demand for multiple simultaneous users of this product? If Internet access will be used, is the existing bandwidth adequate to support the anticipated level of demand?
- What level of technical support for maintenance and updating is available in the library? How much support will be needed from the vendor of the electronic resource? Is adequate equipment already available, or will additional equipment or an upgrade need to be purchased for this product?

These questions will need to be answered before talking with vendors and previewing available electronic resources. In some cases, in a particular subject area, there may be only one product which is only available in one format. This is often not the case, and there may be several competing products available. It will be important to find out what the differences are in coverage: i.e., does one product cover more historical material but include fewer journals than a competitor? How user-friendly are the interfaces? What customer support, training, and technical updates are available?

The currency of the information may be of critical concern. Some vendors update their material more frequently than others, and online formats can be updated more quickly than printed or CD-ROM which must be produced and mailed to the customer. If the database will need to be updated in the library, are there staff members who can be trained and made available to do this?

In addition to the criteria described above, it is also worthwhile to maintain a watchful eye for electronic resources which become available at no charge over the Internet. In reviewing such resources it is important to determine whether they will remain free or if they are being offered at no cost for an initial start-up period only. It is also important to determine if the scope and coverage are equivalent to the commercial product or, if not, the coverage is adequate for a particular library's needs. It may also be that the data are available for free over the Internet, but the search engine and interface are so poor that the information is not nearly as accessible as it is via one of the commercial products. One product that was available commercially at the time that SIBL opened was NetPhone, which provided access to personal and business addresses and telephone numbers in the United States. The same information is now available at no charge (with advertising) over the Internet at http://www.infospaceinc.com/.

THE EXAMPLE OF SIBL

The Science, Industry and Business Library (SIBL) of The New York Public Library (NYPL) opened to the public on May 2nd, 1996.[2] SIBL's collections combine the circulating collection of the Mid-Manhattan Branch of NYPL in science and business with the extensive collections in those areas from the Research Libraries of NYPL. These collections include all areas of basic and applied science (except clinical medicine); business, economics, and international trade; government documents; and patents. Formats include print, microforms, and electronic resources. These materials are housed on 31 miles of compact shelving.

Several years before SIBL opened, the Research Libraries and the Mid-Manhattan Library began to make CD-ROM databases available to the public on standalone workstations and over local area networks. At SIBL, however, the goal was to provide public access to over 100 databases, including commercial as well as government products.

A year prior to the opening of SIBL, an Electronic Collection Development Team was established, including the Assistant Director for Collection Development, the Assistant Director for Access Services, the Assistant Director for Electronic Resources, and the Head of Reference. The first step was a review of the current collection development policy to determine key subject areas which should be covered by electronic databases. A schedule for review of these subject areas was established, and subject specialists from the Reference Department were invited to attend the team's meeting on appropriate dates. The team met every other week for several months to establish the list of "opening day" electronic resources.

When the team met to review each subject area, they were presented with possible choices for databases. In this second phase, the focus was on selection of the databases themselves, not the specific database product. This was done in the attempt to assure balance in the collection and coverage of the most important subject areas.

The third phase involved the selection, for each product, of the vendor and access method or media. These decisions were based on cost, on the technical infrastructure of SIBL, and on the expected level of use of the product. Vendors were invited to make presentations and in some cases it was possible to preview the databases for trial periods. In these cases, the databases were made available and library staff were invited to review and give comments. These three phases were completed several months before the opening of the new library so that there would be time to place the orders. The actual installation of the new products was completed just prior to opening.

The formats that were finally selected included CD-ROM products on stand-alone workstations where indicated either by the level of anticipated demand or by the high cost of a network license. Many other CD-ROM products were licensed for network access, and were loaded in large CD-ROM towers. There were also a number of products which were accessed via the Internet, such as Dow Jones, NEXIS, and the General Business File (InfoTrac) from UMI. These products are updated very frequently and are available at SIBL under flat rate agreements with the vendors. Three Wilson databases (Wilson Business Abstracts, General Science Abstracts, and Applied Science and Technology Abstracts) were tape loaded on a server at the NYPL using software licensed from OCLC (SiteSearch).

All of the networked databases are accessed via HTML menus on designated computers in the Electronic Information Center (EIC.) These menus include broad categories of databases such as "business," "science," "patents," and "government," and there is also a link to a complete alphabetical list of all databases. All of the databases available at SIBL, networked or not, are listed on the menus so that users will have a complete list of all of the resources. Those databases that can be searched over the network are given a hypertext link which launches a batch file which then launches the database. Descriptions of each database are also given.

The EIC is located on the lower level of SIBL, and is the main access point for the electronic databases and the Internet. The complete list of electronic resources available at SIBL is published on the Web at http://www.nypl.org/research/sibl/.

TRAINING IN THE USE OF ELECTRONIC RESOURCES

At SIBL, training for the staff and for the public was critical to the success of the project. Training for SIBL staff was aided by a grant from the Kellogg Foundation, and this funding made possible staff training in basic computer skills, Internet and Web page production, and the hiring of a consultant who facilitated team building and design of a mission statement and goals for the new library. Staff training also included an "adopt-a-CD" program, under which each reference librarian "adopted" a CD-ROM product, studied it in detail, prepared a summary sheet for staff and patrons, and made presentations to the staff on the use of the product.

One of the outstanding features of SIBL is its training facility. Five rooms, four of which have workstations for student use, are available for staff and public training. In four of the rooms, the instructors' lecterns include computer projection, video tape projection, and cable TV.

An instructional program for the public was developed by the reference librarians under the direction of Ann Thornton, Training Coordinator. These courses are offered daily at no cost to the attendees. There is some limited advance registration, but the majority of seats are available on a first-come-first-serve basis on the day of the class. There has been enormous demand for these classes and the evaluations have been highly positive. One user told me that she was sure that she was successful in her job search because of the computer and database skills that she had learned in these classes.

The classes include general information about using SIBL, specialized courses in certain subject areas such as government documents, patent searching, and information for small business owners. Other courses focus on specific databases or databases in particular subject areas. There is also an introductory course in database searching and two sequential courses about the Web. These have been, perhaps, the most popular courses. In the Web courses, the instructors not only teach the basics of what's on the Web and how to find it, but also review ways in which to evaluate Web resources and judge their accuracy and authority. A complete list of courses and a current schedule are available at http://www.nypl.org/research/sibl/.

Among the challenges of teaching these courses has been the wide variation in computer expertise among those who sign up. There have been scientists, librarians, and highly computer-savvy people in the classes, as well as senior citizens and others who have never used computers before. There are several techniques which the staff developed to cope with these challenges: it is most helpful to have an assistant present who can help those who are not quite able to keep up with the rest of the class. Anyone who is hard of hearing or has vision problems is encouraged to sit in the front row near the instructor for extra assistance. Handouts are produced from the PowerPoint slides which form the basis of each class structure, and these handouts are helpful for students in following the class and in later review of what was covered. By developing a standard Power-Point presentation for each course, a number of different librarians are able to teach the same course while maintaining some consistency in the material that is covered. After SIBL had been open a short while, all of the reference librarians were teaching at least one course per week.

CONCLUSION

SIBL has been both praised and criticized for its emphasis on electronic resources. The praise has been rightly deserved for the vision of SIBL's planning and scope, and for its objective of providing the public with electronic access to the most current business and science resources. The criticisms focus on issues of accessibility of materials that are available only in electronic format. It is not always the library's choice: sometimes the materials *are* only available in electronic format, or the electronic format is so vastly superior, more up-to-date, and easier to use than the printed equivalent that access would be severely hampered by providing the printed resource alone. Others argue that there are serious difficulties for the non-computer literate in gaining access to these materials. The training program is an attempt to address this issue, as well as several college students ("Computer Pages") who are employed by SIBL to assist patrons in the use of the electronic resources in the EIC. Finally, SIBL has been criticized for "removing" its journals and books.[3] There are only 60,000 volumes in the open shelf reference collection, 40,000 volumes in the circulating collection, 110,000 serial titles, and 1.2 million volumes in the stacks upstairs!

REFERENCES

1. Samuel Demas, "Collection Development for the Electronic Library: A Conceptual and Organizational Model," *Library Hi Tech* 12 (1994): 71-80.

2. Esther Harriott, "New York's New Door to the Information Age," *American Libraries* 27 (June/July 1996): 58-59.

3. Ingrid Eisenstadter, "A Tangled Info Web," 129 *Newsweek* (February 17, 1997): 16.

A Catalogue of Catalogs:
A Resource for a Small Library
So It Can Be the Place to Go
for Those Who Need to Know

John Christenson

SUMMARY. Information is a critical asset for the success of economic, social and government development in rural America. This article is a current list of information resources for the small town and its library. Categories of information included in this "Catalogue of Catalogs" are rural economic development, antiques and collectibles, agriculture online, agricultural books and videos, do it yourself, rural education, rural health, small business, and small governments. Since rural libraries can be the links in improving rural access to the information superhighway, many of the resources in this article are Internet web sites. Other resources are free and inexpensive pamphlets, paper catalogs, books, magazines and videos suitable for small libraries in rural communities. Most of the resources cannot be found in regular library review journals but are located in municipal county and state government affiliated publications and on web sites specializing in access to rural topics. *[Article copies available for a fee from The Haworth Document Delivery Service: 1-800-342-9678. E-mail address: getinfo@haworthpressinc.com]*

John Christenson is affiliated with the Traverse des Sioux Library System, 110 South Broad Street, Mankato, MN 56001.

[Haworth co-indexing entry note]: "A Catalogue of Catalogs: A Resource for a Small Library So It Can Be the Place to Go for Those Who Need to Know." Christenson, John. Co-published simultaneously in *The Acquisitions Librarian* (The Haworth Press, Inc.) No. 20, 1998, pp. 131-149; and: *Public Library Collection Development in the Information Age* (ed: Annabel K. Stephens) The Haworth Press, Inc., 1998, pp. 131-149. Single or multiple copies of this article are available for a fee from The Haworth Document Delivery Service [1-800-342-9678, 9:00 a.m. - 5:00 p.m. (EST). E-mail address: getinfo@haworthpressinc.com].

RESOURCES FOR THE SMALL TOWN LIBRARY

This resource list for rural and small town libraries is a mixture of catalogs, bibliographies and Internet web sites with connections to a vast multitude of information sources. The list has been compiled as a guide to current pamphlets, videos, books, magazines, and electronic resources which meet the information needs of farmers, ranchers, main street businesses, town museums and tourist centers, rural developers, community health and wellness providers, small schools, volunteer firefighters, elected officials and employees of villages, small towns and townships–including librarians.

Small libraries can never actually own all the useful resources that are available but they can easily provide access to countless informational troves. The sophisticated state and regional interlibrary loan networks developed over the last decade, and now the easy access to electronic resources available through the Internet, enable even the smallest library in the most isolated community to be positioned at the busiest crossroads of the "Information Superhighway."

There is never enough recognition in any community of the basic fact that the town's public library is the only facility funded by public dollars to collect, classify, and disseminate information freely to all citizens. Often this basic premise isn't even recognized by the local librarian who may not always go beyond traditional book and paper resources in the quest for information. Many city councils, planning boards, public works departments, chambers of commerce, main street merchants, volunteer fire departments, farmers, water boards, community economic development committees, and even library boards, will pay extravagant fees to outside consultants and development firms for information that may well have been located through the local library.

The topics that these groups are interested in are the subject areas that are generally not reviewed in library publications. Agriculture, small town government, how-to-do-it, rural education, small business basics, emergency and police training, rural economic development, and local tourism are subjects not usually addressed in the commonly used book selection tools.

Almost twenty years ago, as a director of a regional library service agency serving a rural population in nine south central Minnesota counties, and as a newly elected mayor of Good Thunder, a small farming town of five hundred, I started collecting catalogs and bibliographies of free and unique materials in these elusive subject areas. After I became chair of my county's Small Cities Economic Development Commission, I learned that local officials in neighboring towns were paying thousands of dollars for information that could have been located through any public library. As a mayor working with rural developers and county planners, I became aware of valuable information resources that usually found their way to the bottom drawer of a city clerk's file cabinet but never to the shelves of the town's library where they could have been used over and over again by local citizens.

Consequently, I put together a twelve-page booklet, "A Catalogue of Catalogs: A Resource for a Small Library So It Can Be the Place to Go for Those Who Need to Know." It went through four editions before I stopped compiling it. I used it as the basis for presentations on public relations and community awareness for small libraries that I delivered to rural librarians in more than twelve states.

The last edition of the "Catalogue of Catalogs" was issued in 1988, just as the current electronic information revolution got underway. In that 1988 list there were many more catalogs and references to 16mm films than there were to software programs. Only one citation was completely focused on the new computerized media, "Doane's Agricultural Computing Directory," which listed farm computers, electronic ag networks, and agricultural education software packages.

When I looked at that 1988 list in preparing this new resource list, I found a surprisingly high percentage of citations that are still valid but have now added World Wide Web Internet access. Many of them, including staid organizations such as the National Gardening Association, actually make it very difficult for the searcher to find their "snail-mail" addresses. Ironically, the Lehman Hardware and Appliances website which specializes in hundreds of non-electric appliances, asks that customers not use or request their attractive and expensive-to-print paper catalog, but order items online from their electronic catalog which includes Amish clothing and merchandise.

Organizations such as the National Small Flows Clearinghouse, which offered just five pamphlets on wastewater treatment by mail nine years ago, now has electronic links to dozens of related web sites. It also provides a bibliographic database with abstracts of more than four thousand articles.

Ten years ago there were very few information sources available for country people on the topics of rural health, public safety and emergency services, tourism, telecommunication, alternative farming, and minority education. The Internet revolution is bringing appropriate information in fairly obscure topics to people in the most remote of rural areas.

Many electronic sites and paper bibliographies were searched in updating and developing this rural "Catalogue of Catalogs." The most useful were the National Agriculture Library's "Rural Information Center" (*URL: www.nal.usda.gov/ric*); "The Farmer's Guide to the Internet," a 330-page book produced by TVA-Rural Studies and Farm Journal; "The Internet Guide for Agriculturists," published by John Deere, and "Rural Resources on the Internet," published by the Illinois State Library. Complete ordering information for these publications can be found in the following list under "For a Small Town and Its Library" and "Agriculture Online."

FOR A SMALL TOWN AND ITS LIBRARY

The open-to-all tax-funded public library is the most obvious local city or county institution to be its community's prime source for essential information. Some of the kinds of information that libraries can provide to the local power structure include main street renovation strategies, volunteer firefighter training videos, tourism development ideas, and solutions to waste-water treatment problems. The city clerk, fire chief, planning commission members, and the mayor will more readily support the library's annual budget request when the library repeatedly finds and provides the information needed for improving delivery of municipal services and community betterment.

Agricultural Libraries Information Notes. National Agriculture Library, U.S. Department of Agriculture, Beltsville, MD 20705. Free newsletter published monthly which "provides a channel of communication to technical information for librarians, extension workers, researchers, and scientists in agricultural information activities." Each issue has a listing of Quick Bibliographies and Special Reference Briefs of agricultural and rural topics. Many of these useful publications are online in full text at the NAL web site URL: www.nal.usda.gov. National Agriculture Library has also published a free twenty-four-page guide to Internet resources, "Some Interlibrary Sites on the Internet," by Carol A. Singer.

American Association for State and Local History (AASLH), 530 Church Street, Suite 600, Nashville, TN 37219-2325. URL: www.aaslh.org is a complete catalog of materials online with links to individual state historical societies and museums. AASLH is a publisher and distributor of a wealth of books, videos, and pamphlets about small museum management, local history research, and small town preservation.

American Planning Association Planners Book Service. American Planning Association, 1313 East 60th Street, Chicago, IL 60537. Sixty-page free catalog of books for city clerks, mayors, city managers, and planners in zoning, historic preservation, rural and small town planning, and municipal services. URL: www.planning.org/books/ bookstar.html lists all books and provides one-stop ordering process. A new page, "Cybarbia: The Planning and Architecture Internet Resource Center," is a comprehensive directory of Internet resources relevant to planning, architecture, urbanism, and small towns listing 5,527 links.

Center for the Study of Rural Librarianship. College of Library Science, Clarion University of Pennsylvania, Clarion, PA 16214. Publisher of the semiannual journal "Rural Libraries" ($5/issue), a forum for rural library service. Also publishes bibliographies relating to rural librarianship.

Country-Net. A down-home guide to the Internet for grown-ups living in Rural America. URL: www.lyon-lincolnet.com/martyg/ cindex.htm.

Fire Fighting. URL: www.nerdworld.com/nw656.html. More than one hundred links to information resources for firefighters.

Fire Fighter's Bookstore. 18281 Gothard, #105, Huntington Beach, CA 92648-1205. Ninety-page catalog of books, videos, and software for the entire fire service. Web page at URL: www.firebooks.com.

Heartland Center for Leadership Development, 941 'O' Street, Suite 920, Lincoln, NE 68508. URL: www.4w.com/heartland/ Heartland's publications are called "Resources for Small Town Survival" and can be ordered online as well as by mail.

International City/County Management Association, 777 North Capitol Street NE, Washington, DC 20002-4201. Publisher and distributor of books and correspondence training programs on a wide variety of local government management, financing and planning subjects. URL: www.icma.org.

Media Resources, Inc., 2614 Fort Vancouver Way, Vancouver, WA 98661. Free catalog of one hundred videocassettes suitable for volunteer fire department and emergency responder training.

Miscellaneous Rural Homepage. URL: rip.physics.unk.edu/rural/rural.html. Hundreds of links to online rural resources.

National Association of Towns and Townships (NATaT), 449 North Capitol Street NW, Suite 294, Washington, DC 20001. Publishes ten guidebooks useful for small town officials, some with accompanying video programs. NATaT also sponsors a National Center for Small Communities to assist local officials in providing public services. URL: sso.org/natat/natat.htm.

National Drinking Water Clearinghouse, PO Box 6064, West Virginia University, Morgantown, WV 26506-6064. Offers one hundred fifty free or low cost informational products including brochures, videos, and government publications which assist small communities in dealing with drinking water issues. URL: www.estd.wvu.edu/ndwc/ndwc_homepage.html. All informational products can be ordered online.

National Fire Protection Association, Publication Sales Division, Batterymarch Park, PO Box 9101, Quincy, MA 02269-9101. Publisher of eight hundred technical and educational materials on all aspects of fire safety. URL: www.nfpa.org/ provides hundreds of links constituting a virtual reference library of fire resources.

National Main Street Center Publications and Audiovisual Materials. National Trust for Historic Preservation, 1785 Massachusetts Avenue NW, Washington, DC 20036. List of manuals, slide shows, videocassettes and other materials on downtown revitalization. URL: www.mainst.org/bookstore/bookstoremain.htm. Materials can be ordered online.

National Small Flows Clearinghouse, PO Box 6064, West Virginia University, Morgantown, WV 26506-6064. Offers a number of wastewater-related informational products for small communities including case studies, computer searches, design manuals, fact sheets, videos, and technology packages. URL: www.estd.wvu.edu/nsfc/nsfc_home page.html. All informational products can be ordered online.

The Police Officer's Internet Directory. URL: www.officer.com. Hundreds of police related links.

Promoting Tourism in Rural America. URL: ourtown.sunrem.com/ourtown/brochure/toc.html. Fifty-six annotated titles of articles on rural tourism are listed.

Reiman Publications, 5400 South 60th Street, Greendale, WI 53129. The publisher of the very popular "Country Woman," "Reminisce," "Birds and Bloom," and "Country" magazines also has a trade catalog of over fifty books featuring nostalgia, rural and down-home cooking titles.

RELIC (Rural Electronic Library Information Center) URL:www. norweld.lib.oh.us/2_re.htm. Links to Rural Internet Resources as well as information on subscribing to the "Rural Library Services Newsletter" published by NORWELD, Northwest Library District, 251 North Main Street, Bowling Green, OH 43402.

Rural Information Center (RIC). URL: www.nal.usda.gov/ric/. The ultimate rural information center located in the USDA's National Agricultural Library, 10301 Baltimore Boulevard, Room 304, Beltsville, MD 20705-2351. RIC provides information and referral services about all things rural for local government, libraries, cooperatives, businesses and rural citizens. Publications include QB (Quick Bibliography on a specific rural topic) and the Rural Information Center Publication Series.

Rural Resources on the Internet. URL: www.gridley.org/~bradneal/ rural.html. The on-line version of the Illinois State Library's thirty-page booklet "Rural Resources on the Internet: A Pathfinder." This booklet for librarians assisting their rural patrons in gaining access to electronic information is available free from the Illinois State Library, 300 S. Second Street, Springfield, IL 62701-1976.

Septic System Information Web Site. URL: www.inspect-ny.com/ septbook.htm. Expert sources for septic tank and wastewater information from the American Society of Home Inspectors.

Small Town, Small Towns Institute, PO Box 517, Ellensburg, WA 98926. Semi-monthly magazine, $35. New ideas and resources for citizens and officials of small communities. Small Town published excellent *Design Resource Book for Small Communities* (96 pages, 1981, $10) and *Historic Preservation Resource Book for Small Communities* (100 pages, 1983, $10).

World Wide Web of Emergency Services. URL: dumbo.isc.rit.edu/ ems/wwwes.html. A guide to the wealth of emergency services (EMS) information available online.

RURAL ECONOMIC DEVELOPMENT

Practical rural economic development ideas usually cannot be located in the books filling the shelves of small town libraries. However, the Internet can provide links to hundreds of resources on paper and online. This is the type of information that is often sold to small communities by developers and civil engineers at high cost. They simply locate much of it at government agencies including large libraries.

Applied Rural Telecommunications. Colorado Advanced Technology Institute, 1025 Broadway, Suite 700, Denver, CO 80202. An online economic development resource center and rural telecom resource guide at URL: bcn.boulder.co.us/aerie.

Extending Internet Resources for Rural Development. Hot links to hundreds of resources in rural topics such as telecommunication, economic development, and service information. URL:www.ag.uiuc.edu/~mullen/rural/tester 4.html.

Midwest Research Institute, 425 Volker Boulevard, Kansas City, MO 64110-2299. Publisher of a dozen titles in rural economic development. URL: www.mriresearch.org/weblinks.html has links to many rural economic development tools.

RUPRI: Rural Development Centers. This URL: www.rupri.org/rudevcnt.html has links to all four regional rural development centers supporting research and extension efforts to improve the lives of people living in rural areas. Each center publishes a free monthly newsletter with at least one page devoted to a list of pertinent publications in the area of rural development. Each center's web site lists all of the center's publications and provides links with other rural development sites.

Rural Development Perspectives, Superintendent of Documents, U.S. Government Printing Office, Washington, DC 20402. (Three times a year, $10). An eclectic mix of information, ideas, and issues of concern to rural America.

USDA Rural Development. URL: www.rurdev.usda.gov. Links to economic development resources on the Internet from the U.S. Office of Rural Development.

The W.K. Kellogg Collection of Rural Community Development Resources. URL: www.unl.edu/kellogg/index.html. This is a library of high quality rural community development materials funded by the Kellogg Foundation. An annotated bibliography of the collection is on the web site. This Heartland Center project is located at the University of Nebraska.

FOR MAIN STREET BUSINESSES

Most of the business materials covered by library review tools are primarily suitable for large library business and investment collections. About ten years ago there were several comprehensive reference books of annotated listings of small business resources. Although most of these titles are out-of-print, there are now many appropriate WWW sites which have links to paper and online resources for those small businesses on Main Street, USA.

IBM Small Business Connection Home Page at URL: www.sbaon line.sba.gov. This federal government site has online information on all aspects of small business operations and "great business hot-links" to another 2,076 useful sites.

Inc. Online. The electronic version of INC. magazine at URL: www.inc.com. A wealth of current online resources for the small business operator including over one hundred useful business links.

Small Business Advancement National Center (SBANC). Located at the University of Central Arkansas in Conway, AR, the SBANC houses down-loadable research information on all aspects of small business, links to resources and a listserv of new information. URL: wwwsbanet.uca.edu/.

Small Business Center. Sponsored by IBM at URL:www.idm.ibm. com. Hints on doing business on the net as well as lists of magazine articles, references, URLs and toll-free numbers useful for small business owners.

Small Business Development Center of Northwest Texas. This SBDC web site provides connections to all the other SBDCs around the nation, links to other business resources and a place to order SBDC micro-guides on business start-up issues at a discount. URL: www.bizcoach.org/.

ANTIQUES AND COLLECTIBLES

People in rural communities are great collectors of "stuff." This may be because sales auctions and town-wide garage sales are regular community social events. For whatever reason, the small town library has great demands for detailed information on obscure collectibles. Web sites and catalogs can help the librarian verify the existence of very specialized information that can be requested on interlibrary loan.

Antiques and Collectibles Resources on the Web. This site, URL: www.autonomy.com/antiques.htm, contains hundreds of appropriate links including the Antiques and Collectibles Bookstore in association with Amazon.Com Books.

Antique Trader Books, 100 Bryant Street, PO Box 1050, Debuque, IA 52003. Publisher of dozens of guides to Americana, collectibles and antiques.

Collector Books, PO Box 3009, Paducah, KY 52002-3009. Free forty-six page catalog of over two hundred books on the art of collecting.

The Vestal Press, Ltd., 4720 Boston Way, Lanham, MD 20706. Publisher and distributor of a delightful collection of seven hundred fifty diversified subjects including mechanical music, railroads, old radios, bicycles and wooden boats.

Wallace-Homestead, 201 King of Prussia Road, Radnor, PA 19089. A variety of collecting guide books and rural nostalgia items.

AGRICULTURE ONLINE

There are literally thousands of URLs related to farming, crops, market and price information, and livestock. The following general agricultural-related sites and book resources will provide leads and access to specific topics from alternative agriculture to soybean promotion.

Agriculture Home Page. This web site at URL: www.cs.fsu.edu/projects/group3/agri.html links together many, many sources of agricultural information available on the World Wide Web.

@Griculture Online. The home page of *Successful Farming* magazine which has links to many commercial ag sites. URL: www.agriculture.com.

Agrigator. The University of Florida's colorful index of agricultural and related information on a constantly updated site at URL: gnv.ifas.ufl.edu/WWW/AGATOR/HTM/AG.HTM.

Alternative Farming Systems Information Center. Locates and accesses information related to non-conventional cropping systems. A USDA National Agricultural Library Information Center at URL: www.nal.usda.gov/afsic.

The Farmer's Guide to the Internet by Henry James. TVA Rural Studies, 400 Agricultural Engineering Bldg., The University of Kentucky, Lexington, KY 40546-0276, 2nd edition, 1996. $19.95. 334 pages. A joint TVA-*Farm Journal* project designed to help first-time users to start up and run quickly on the Net. Includes extensive listing of thousands of agricultural sites including weather, markets and pricing, livestock and crops. An online update is located at URL: www.rural.org/Farmers_Guide/.

The Internet Guide for Agriculturists by Jim Grozinger. John Deere Publishing, Dept. 374, Moline, IL 61265-8098, 1997. $27.95. 64 pages. This very practical introduction is appropriately subtitled "Helping you to plow your way through all the information on the World Wide Web." Features full-color illustrations of screen examples of sites, browsers, and e-mail providers.

Not Just Cows. This site, URL: www.snymor.edu/~drewwe/njc, is a basic index to dozens of agricultural resources. A unique site that actually moos at the visitor.

Penpages. The Pennsylvania State University College of Agricultural Sciences home page provides full-text information relating to agricultural sciences, forest resources and community development displaying thirteen thousand current items of information at URL: www.penpages.psu.edu.

U.S. Department of Agriculture at URL: www.usda.gov. Hundreds of rural and agriculturally related web sites.

Websidestory World's Top 1000 Pages-Agriculture. One hundred eclectic ag web sites at URL: www.hitbox.com/wc/MAKElists/top100 Agriculture.html.

World Wide Web Virtual Library: Agriculture. Links to virtually any ag topic at URL: ipmwww.ncsu.edu/cernag/cern.html.

Yahoo!-Science: Agriculture. An exhaustive list of ag links at URL: www.yahoo.com/Science/Agriculture.

AGRICULTURAL BOOKS AND VIDEOS

The topic of agriculture has the least number of books published each year in the annual listing in "Publisher's Weekly" by subject area. This small group of "ag" books is seldom reviewed but there are many descriptive free publisher catalogs available for selection purposes.

AAVIM, Engineering Center, University of Georgia, Athens, GA 30602. The American Association for Vocational Instructional Materials publishes some basic vocational technical titles in the field of agriculture.

ASAE, Dept. 9987, St. Joseph, MI 49085-9659. The American Society of Agricultural Engineers catalog of old farm equipment books features classic inexpensive reprints of early farm machinery literature. Also lists videos of early farm equipment. URL: asae.org. includes publication catalog, and an index to technical articles in eleven agricultural engineering periodicals and 5,500 unpublished ASAE papers.

Cooperative Extension Services. Each state's Cooperative Extension has a catalog of free and inexpensive publications in the fields of agriculture, economic development, families, gardening, homemaking, and rural development. Most of the Extensions have also developed web pages that not only list publications but provide many of them online in full text. The U.S. Department of Agriculture's Cooperative State Research Education and Extension Service has a web site, URL: www.reeusda.gov/statepartners/usa.htm, with a United States map which leads to extension web sites in all fifty states.

Diamond Farm Book Publishers, PO Box 537, Alexandria Bay, NY 13607. Good listing of varied farming titles including antique equipment, shop manuals and collectibles. URL: www.diamondfarm.com/genstore.htm. An online general store with annotations and full color illustrations of more than one hundred books and videos.

Interstate Home Page, 19-27 North Jackson Street, Danville, IL 61832. The "Approved Practices" series is published by Interstate as well as AgriScience text books. URL: www.ippinc.com.

Iowa State University Press, 2121 South State Avenue, Ames, IA 50014-8300. Good farming and rural titles can be found at www.iastate.edu/help/m/isupress.html.

John Deere Publications, John Deere Road, Moline, IL 61265. Books, videotapes, software and slide sets on agricultural machinery and agribusiness management. URL: www.deere.com/aboutus/pub/jdpub/. Includes a quarterly newsletter and annotated listing of sales materials.

Midwest Plan Service, 122 Davidson Hall, Iowa State University, Ames, IA 50011-3080. Catalog lists twenty pages of handbooks and building guides for the farmer. These low-cost publications are available through all midwestern state university Agricultural Engineering Departments and county extension offices.

Merck & Company, Box 2000, Rahway, NJ 07065. Veterinary books.

Motorbooks International, PO Box 1, Osceola, WI 54020. Offers reprints of old farm machinery manuals and catalogs.

New Books, U.S. Government Printing Office, Washington, DC 20402. Monthly. Free. Occasionally lists new rural titles for sale by Superintendent of Documents under "Agriculture" subject heading. For access to paper and electronic government information on the web use URL: www.access.gpo.gov/su-docs/index.html.

Rodale Press, Inc., 33 East Minor Street, Emmaus, PA 18098. Farming, gardening, how-to-do-it, cookbooks and homesteading books from the publisher of "Organic Gardening." URL: www.rodale

press.com. is an online bookstore featuring almost five hundred titles.

Storey Publishing, 105 Schoolhouse Road, Pownal, VT 05261. How-to books for country living can be ordered at URL: www. storey.com.

Videos for Farmers from Your Public Library. Traverse des Sioux Library System, PO Box 608, Mankato, MN 56002-0608. A free annotated listing of more than fifty agricultural videocassettes available for loan, and inter-library loan, from Traverse des Sioux.

WINNCO, PO Box 397, Quitman, TX 75783-0397. 1-800-494-6626. A four-page listing of small farm and rural books sold by this distributor who specializes in dealing with schools and libraries.

DOING IT YOURSELF

There are several old-time book publishers offering contemporary titles on the basics of home improvement and carpentry, but there are not many online resources.

American Technical Publishers, 12235 S. Laramie Avenue, Alsip, IL 60658. Carpentry and construction books.

Audel, Bobbs Merrill Company, PO Box 7083, Indianapolis, IN 46206. Basic books in such areas as house wiring, plumbing, carpentry, welding and small engine repair.

Builders Booksource, 1801 Fourth Street, Berkeley, CA 94710. Remarkably complete online catalog of books having to do with building based on a full bookstore's collection. URL: www.buildersbook site.com is a useful website for selection and ordering.

Lindsay's Technical Books. Lindsay Publications, Inc., PO Box 12, Bradley, IL 60915-0012. Eighty-five pages of new and reprint books in two hundred subject areas including tool making, wood working, steam engineering, blacksmithing and welding.

Meredith Books, Book Customer Service, 1716 Locust Street, Des Moines, IA 50309-3023. Free catalog of hundreds of books from

Better Homes and Gardens, Ortho, and Meredith with home improvement, gardens and doing-it-yourself titles.

NCAT–The National Center for Appropriate Technology, PO Box 3838, Butte, MT 59702. Booklets, bibliographies, plans and books on renewable energy, sustainable agriculture, and technology exchange. Online at URL: www.ncat.org/.

Sams–Howard W. Sams, 201 West 103rd Street, Indianapolis, IN 46290. General hobby and how-to-do-it, particularly electronic equipment manuals. URL: www.hwsams.com/sams_model_new.html. allows online search of database of 150,000 products.

Sunset Books, Lane Publishing Company, Willow and Middlefield Roads, Menlo Park, CA 94025. Attractive building, remodeling, home design, gardening, hobby and cookbooks at reasonable prices.

Tab Books, Inc., Blue Ridge Summit, PA 17214. Six hundred fifty titles of how to repair, build, strip down, remodel, and understand most any perplexing mechanical or electronic thing. Latest catalog moves into computers, video and software. Also publisher of "Self-Counsel Press" books aimed at the small business person.

Technical Publications Division, Intertec Publishing Corp., PO Box 12901, Overland Park, KS 66212. One hundred thirty service manuals for engines, tractors, outboard motors, lawnmowers, chainsaws, generators, snowmobiles, and other equipment. Publisher of the *invaluable* I & T Shop Service Manuals for most makes and models of farm tractors.

SEED CATALOGS

Since people living in small towns and rural communities have more land available to them, they often put it into gardens. Most of the information that gardeners receive comes from neighbors, the local hardware or garden supply store, extension services and seed catalogs. These catalogs contain a wealth of important planting and growing hints wrapped in colorful pictures of flowers, herbs, and vegetables. Seed catalogs are usually mailed out in the week between Christmas and New Year, just in time for cold weather dreams of spring planting. Because every rural resident receives seed catalogs, a small library can be an exchange point for dozens of exotic and specialized catalogs.

Garden Gate. URL: www.prairienet.org/garden-gate/. A well organized collection of links to seed catalogs, gardening books, garden supply catalogs, mailing lists, gardening CD-ROMS and videos, and Rot Web, a web site devoted to composting at URL: net.indra. com/~topsoil/Compost_Menu.html.

Seed Savers Yearbook. Seed Savers Exchange, 3076 North Winn Road, Decorah, IA 52101. Lists 11,898 unique varieties of non-hybrid vegetable seeds available from the Seed Savers Heritage Farm and members at a minimal cost. The annual Inventory is included in the annual $25 membership to Seed Savers Exchange. You will also receive newsletters, a yearbook, two issues of a hundred page magazine, a "Flower and Herb Exchange" service and a "Plant Finder Service."

National Gardening Association. URL: www2.garden.org/nga/home. html. Features online directory to mail-order gardening and seed catalogs with hyperlinks to websites and fast e-mail for ordering. The NGA site also includes a key word search function to its library of magazine articles.

Seed, Bulb, & Nursery Supplies, Reader Service Department, "Organic Gardening," Reader's Service, 33 East Minor Street, Emmaus, PA 18098. Annual ten-page annotated listing of over two hundred seed catalogs. Available by writing at end of the year or early January and sending one dollar.

SERENDIPITY

These catalogs are valuable reference tools for finding hard to locate old time goods and items from past eras. The Whole Earth Catalog reviews materials in practical, but obscure subject areas not indexed in traditional reference resources.

The Catalog of Catalogs: The Complete Mail-Order Directory by Edward L. Palder. Woodbine House, 1997, $24.95. 423 pages. An annotated listing of almost ten thousand catalogs in hundreds of subject categories.

Cumberland General Store "Wish and Want Book." #1 Highway 68, Dept. INT96, Crossville, TN 38555. 228 pages. $4. A cornucopia of practical old time items available hardly anywhere else–six models of surreys with fringe tops (price range $3,675 to $5,275), cast iron wash kettles, sheet mica, seven varieties of butter churns, heavy duty milk cans, brass pitcher pump, and complete horse harness gear. URL: www.opup.org/~sces/store.html.

Lehman's Home Page, PO Box 41, Kidron, OH 44636. 180 pages. $3. Two thousand items used by the Amish and Swiss Mennonite neighbors of Lehman's store in the "Non-Electric Good Neighbor Heritage Catalog." Almost all items can be ordered from the online catalog at www.lehmans.com.

The Millennium Whole Earth Catalog: Access to Tools and Ideas for the Twenty-First Century. Harper, 1995. $30. The newest edition of the famous "Whole Earth Catalog." An evaluation and access tool with more than two thousand intriguing entries covering a vast array of pertinent subjects. A very basic book for any library. A hypertext version is available at www.well.net/mwec.

RURAL EDUCATION

Rural communities benefit in having a good public school located in town far beyond the expected education values. That school is often the largest employer in the city, and its gyms and meeting rooms are where most community-wide events are held. The teachers and administrators are often the best educated residents and many are natural community leaders. The following, mostly online, resources will help the small town librarian locate educational support information for the school district, interested parents, and for community leaders wanting to strengthen public education. Home schoolers often utilize the public library as their own school library and the listed URLs will help the librarian find appropriate resources for their growing and demanding population.

Affordable Access, Rural Online. A nonprofit organization helping rural schools use new information technologies. Many useful links as well as the very latest information on Universal Service for libraries and schools. URL: www.itc.org/aaron/.

Eric/Cress Program Descriptions. ERIC Clearinghouse on Rural Education and Small Schools, Box 3AP, New Mexico State University, Las Cruses, NM 88003. Publisher and resource center for rural school information. Six fact sheets and two CRESS-NOTES news bulletins are published annually and distributed free. URL: aelvira. ael.org/erichp.htm also includes a complete set of clearinghouse digests from 1982 to present. It also has an electronic Native Education Directory with web links. The CRESS site also has links to nearly eighty related rural education organizations.

Farm Country General Store, Route 2, Box 412, Metamora, IL 61542. A ninety-six page catalog of home schooling resources. $2.00. Information and resources available on URL: www.outrig.com/farm country/.

Homeschool Mall. URL: www.home-school.com/HSMall.html. A linkage to hundreds of sites useful to a home schooler.

Rural Clearing House for Lifelong Education and Development. Kansas State University, 101 College Court Building, Manhattan, KS 66506-6001. Publications related to rural education. The URL: www-personal.ksu.edu/~rcled/ has one hundred rural information sites.

Rural Education Association, Colorado State University, 300 Education Bldg., Fort Collins, CO 80523. Newsletters, journals, data, and research to enhance educational opportunities in rural and small school systems. URL: www.colostate.edu/orgs/NREA.

RURAL HEALTH

The most common characteristic of being rural is isolation from basic services, particularly in the areas of health and medicine. The following links will help rural citizens, and their healthcare givers, obtain access to the best in current health information.

Health Web. Links to specific, evaluated health related information resources on the www selected by librarians and information professionals. At URL: healthweb.org/index.html.

Institute for Rural and Environmental Health. An online information resource center located at the University of Iowa, 100 Oakdale Campus #163 AMRF, Iowa City, IA 52242-5000. By submitting an on-line "database search request form," a user can request the Institute to search through a dozen databases, including Medline, for health information topics. URL: info.pmeh.uiowa.edu/.

National Rural Education Association, One West Armour Boulevard, Suite 301, Kansas City, MO 64111. Publishes newsletter, journal, books, brochures, tapes, and videos in the field of rural health. URL: www.nrharural.org/pr.html.

Rural Information Center Health Service (RICHS). Located in the National Agriculture Library, 10301 Baltimore Boulevard, Room 304, Beltsville, MD 20705-2351. RICHS offers brief free database searches on rural health topics, furnishes selected publications, referral services, and links to a wide variety of related www sites. URL: www.nal. usda.gov/ric/richs/. (Includes Hispanic/Latino Health resources in Spanish.)

RuralNet. The Marshall University School of Medicine. Rural Health Resource, Huntington, WV 25755. Links to hundreds of rural health and medical resources. URL: ruralnet.marshall.edu/.

Gay and Lesbian Library Materials:
A Book Selector's Toolkit

Cal Gough
Ellen Greenblatt

SUMMARY. Despite an abundance of books published for lesbian and gay readers, librarians in all types of libraries continue to under-collect these materials. Current tools useful to selectors of lesbigay books are listed, including printed and Internet sources of bibliographic data, subject bibliographies, book reviews, bestseller lists, and lists of award-winning books and authors. The importance of retrospective collecting and periodic inventories is mentioned, and subjects of perennial interest to gay and lesbian readers are listed. The article concludes with a list of essential lesbian and gay reference books. *[Article copies available for a fee from The Haworth Document Delivery Service: 1-800-342-9678. E-mail address: getinfo@haworthpressinc. com]*

The abundance and variety of books written by, for, and about lesbians and gay men has increased enormously within the past 30 years. Neither this abundance nor this variety is reflected in most library collections, however. Recent studies show this to be the case regardless of the type of library collection examined[1] or the availability of reviews for these materials.[2] This persistent, widespread resistance to routinely collecting materi-

Cal Gough is Adult Materials Selection Specialist for the Atlanta-Fulton Public Library, Margaret Mitchell Square, Atlanta, GA 30303. Ellen Greenblatt is Assistant Director for Technical Services at Auraria Library, University of Colorado at Denver, 1100 Lawrence Street, Denver, CO 80204.

[Haworth co-indexing entry note]: "Gay and Lesbian Library Materials: A Book Selector's Toolkit." Gough, Cal and Ellen Greenblatt. Co-published simultaneously in *The Acquisitions Librarian* (The Haworth Press, Inc.) No. 20, 1998, pp. 151-170; and: *Public Library Collection Development in the Information Age* (ed: Annabel K. Stephens) The Haworth Press, Inc., 1998, pp. 151-170. Single or multiple copies of this article are available for a fee from The Haworth Document Delivery Service [1-800-342-9678, 9:00 a.m. - 5:00 p.m. (EST). E-mail address: getinfo@haworthpressinc.com].

151

als of interest or usefulness to lesbian and gay library users is a pattern that could be explained in several ways.[3] This article describes the selection tools currently available to librarians who are willing to undertake a more conscientious effort to collect lesbigay materials.[4]

The depth and breadth of such an effort will vary according to type of library, size of budget, the degree of the selector's knowledge and autonomy, and the amount of time a selector can devote to selecting these materials among the others s/he is responsible for purchasing. On the other hand, regardless of who's doing the collecting, which user groups these efforts are made for, how much or little money there is to spend, or how much or how little time can be devoted to spending it, many of the methods of identifying quality lesbigay materials are the same in virtually every library context. And while there is no single set of reliable formulas or selection methods suitable for selecting lesbigay materials in every type or size of library, there are similar questions that every selector for these materials should ask to determine the most sensible way to improve the quantity and/or quality of lesbigay materials in a particular collection.[5] Before plunging into a focused collection building effort, and regardless of your level of knowledge about the subject,[6] you need to ask yourself a few basic questions about what you can realistically accomplish:

- Are you aiming to quickly increase the sheer total number of lesbigay *titles* in your collection?
- Is it your goal to obtain sufficient *copies* of the most heavily circulated lesbigay items already in your collection?
- Is broadening the range of distinct *topics* addressed by the lesbigay items in your collection what you hope to do?
- Do you hope to increase the *types* of items represented (e.g., genre fiction as well as nonfiction) in your collection?
- Have you decided to identify and purchase lesbigay information in *formats other than books*?[7]
- Are you wanting to give closer scrutiny to guaranteeing the continued *availability* of the items you have already purchased (i.e., making more frequent or more systematic attempts to replace missing items)?
- Do you want to improve *coordination among other selectors* with responsibilities for different parts of your library's collection (i.e., work with colleagues to insure that all of you are routinely ordering lesbigay materials in your respective areas of collection responsibility)?
- Are you simply wanting to become more *systematic* than you have been previously in the way you collect lesbigay materials?

You may decide you are interested in doing more than one of these things. Whatever the scope of the effort, clarity about your goals will save you time and effort by helping you to envision the sequence of steps you need to use in pursuing your goal(s). That in turn will prevent you from becoming overwhelmed at the outset or mired down midway through the project, make it easier for you to communicate to colleagues or supervisors what you're trying to do, and help you devise methods of measuring your progress.

LOCATING BIBLIOGRAPHIC DATA

Due to the discovery during the past decade by mainstream publishers of the lucrative market for lesbigay publications,[8] many of the sources used for identifying and evaluating lesbigay titles are the same ones used for approaching the collecting of materials on other subjects. These standard selection tools will be described below along with others unique to collecting lesbigay materials.

Books in Print

These days, the number of items retrieved from searching this database for titles related to the interests and opinions of lesbians and gay men can be unwieldy. Despite this disadvantage, searching *Books in Print (BIP)* is still the quickest way to generate a list of currently available candidates for purchase. All of us are familiar with the print version of this database, although many of us have discovered the advantages of using instead either an online version or the CD-ROM version (often networked on our computerized catalogs) called *Books in Print Plus*. Selectors using the print version of *BIP* for ordering purposes should pay close attention to checking the long list of cross-references listed at the "Homosexuality" entry, and remember as well to check all these cross-references in *BIP's* annual supplement, *Forthcoming Books*. Selectors of lesbigay materials who have access to the electronic versions of *BIP* (which include the titles in *Forthcoming Books*) can exploit the advantages of searching by keywords instead of by controlled subject terms; using timesaving truncation; creating Boolian searches; and printing out (or downloading) *BIP* records in various formats—including an order format which many libraries allow selectors to submit in lieu of their own order forms. The *BIP Plus* CD is gradually becoming more useful to all book selectors as more excerpts from book reviews or publishers' 200-word descriptions are added to its database of titles, and because selectors can now limit searches to items new to the database since the previous monthly update.[9]

Amazon

Amazon (http:///www.amazon.com) was the first major company to sell books (and audiovisual materials) over the Internet. Its huge inventory is a rich source of bibliographic data that contains many titles not included in *Books in Print*. Some library selectors now routinely search Amazon along with *BIP* when searching for bibliographic or availability information about a particular title. You can search the database at Amazon's exceptionally well-organized Web site by author's name, title, subject, keyword, and ISBN. Boolian searches (e.g., "lesbian AND detective") are also possible. Amazon's "Expert Editors" feature is another time-saver: sign yourself up under the categories "Lesbian Studies and Literature" and "Gay Studies and Literature" and you will receive, at regular intervals, e-mail messages containing reviews of new releases added to Amazon's inventory. (The reviews are currently written by award-winning authors Rebecca Brown and Michael Bronski.)

Other Publishing Resources

As the bibliographic data in publisher and vendor catalogs is usually accompanied by enough descriptive information to make most purchase decisions, one of the most important ways to keep abreast of new lesibgay titles entering the market is to regularly examine the relevant catalogs. The traditional method of doing this is to contact the companies and get your name on their mailing lists. However, as more and more publishers are making their catalogs available on the World Wide Web, library selectors with Internet access can avoid the tedium, wasted paper, and delays associated with signing up for mailing lists by checking cyberspace for publishers' offerings. To locate publishers of lesbigay materials on the Web, consult the directory of Queer Publishers (http://www.cudenver.edu/public/library/libraryq/qpubs.html). This site includes small press publishers as well as major commercial and academic presses. Whichever route you choose, at a minimum you need to routinely review the descriptions of new releases by those publishers responsible for producing the bulk of lesbigay books available to libraries.[10] Additionally, many national and regional book vendors produce special catalogs of their lesbigay titles,[11] and Alamo Square exclusively distributes lesbigay books.[12] There are also a few national organizations dedicated to promoting new lesbigay books.

Useful publisher information (among other things) is available from the Women's Presses Library Project[13] and The Publishing Triangle.[14]

Bookstores as Resources

Lesbian and gay bookstores can also provide valuable information about appropriate titles for library collections. Many of these bookstores produce newsletters, catalogs, and Web pages. To find them, order the printed directory available from the Clearinghouse of the American Library Association's Gay, Lesbian, and Bisexual Task Force[15] or use one of the several bookstore directories on the Internet.[16]

The staff of your local gay, lesbian, or feminist bookstore, if you are fortunate in having one located near your library, are excellent resources for library selectors. As it is their job to know in some detail what's available and what's in demand, an ongoing alliance with someone working in one of these stores can be a real asset in keeping up with trends and titles you might otherwise overlook in the other methods you use to keep your collection up to date.

Feminist Bookstore News (FBN)[17] is a publication directed primarily at bookstore owners, but it can also be extremely useful to library selectors whose libraries can afford a subscription. Published every other month, *FBN* contains information on 250 to 350 new books in each issue. Although its primary focus is feminist books, *FBN* has long included a column called "Gay Men's Lit." The publisher's annual "Feminist Bookstores' Catalog" highlights new releases of interest.

Online Bibliographic Utilities

The electronic resources maintained by the Online Computer Library Center (OCLC)[18] and the Research Library Information Network (RLIN)[19] are useful to library selectors needing bibliographic information about lesbigay titles or wanting to know how many other libraries (or which particular libraries, or which type of libraries) have already purchased a particular title. WorldCat, the end-user version of OCLC's union catalog, and Eureka, the end-user version of RLIN's, can both be easily searched by author, title, subject, and keyword. The searcher can limit retrieval by date, language, and format.

Library Catalogs on the Internet

Selectors gathering bibliographic or library holdings information about lesbigay materials may occasionally need to supplement their searches of

OCLC and RLIN by using the Internet to check the catalogs of other libraries in the United States with significant collections of lesbigay materials. These library catalogs, all searchable both by keyword and by subject heading, include:

- San Francisco Public Library (telnet://206.14.7.103).
- Hennepin County Library (Web (Java-based telnet): http://www.hennepin.lib.mn.us/ or telnet://hennepin.lib.mn.us; at the login: prompt, type the word *library*).
- the University of Washington Library (Web: http://www.lib.washington.edu/ or telnet://uwin.u.washington.edu).
- Princeton University Library (Web (Java-based telnet): http://library.princeton.edu/databases/catalog-java.html or telnet://library.princeton.edu:4028).

Something to keep in mind when searching library catalogs by subject heading (rather than keyword) is that most large public and academic libraries (Hennepin County Library being the most notable exception) catalog their materials, including lesbigay materials, with subject headings devised by the Library of Congress. These terms (like terms from any controlled vocabulary) can be rather difficult to remember. If you seem to be having trouble retrieving the number of titles you expect, you may want to consult the current list of lesbigay LC subject headings maintained by John DeSantis on the Internet at http://carbon.cudenver.edu/public/library/libq/qsubj.html.

CARL UnCover Books-in-Reveal

If your library subscribes to the UnCover Reveal Service, you may (especially if you work in an academic library) want to consider using its new Books-in-Reveal service to alert you about new books of lesbigay interest.[20] On a weekly basis, this service uses search terms specified by the user to search titles in the Academic Book Center's Approval Plan and alerts the user by e-mail of any matches.

Electronic Discussion Lists as Resources

Participation in electronic discussion lists is an easy way for librarians with Internet access to network with other selectors of lesbigay books. New releases, Web sites of interest, and articles about lesbigay librarianship are often mentioned or discussed on these lists. Two lists of particular interest are GAY-LIBN: The Gay/Lesbian/Bisexual Librarians Network[21] and LEZBRIAN: The Lesbian and Bisexual Women Library Workers List.[22]

SUBJECT BIBLIOGRAPHIES

The explosion of lesbigay publishing during the past ten years or so has virtually foreclosed the possibility of comprehensive or near-comprehensive bibliographic control of lesbigay books.[23] Narrowly-focused lesbigay subject bibliographies are plentiful, however. For a sampling of the most recent lists, most of them annotated, in library journals, check *Library Literature*. (If you use the print version, look for the subheading "Homosexuality" under the main heading "Book Lists." Keyword searching is possible in the electronic versions.) Check *Bibliographic Index* (again, either the print version or an electronic one) for references to bibliographies published in journals outside "Libraryland."

Special-topic lists–some annotated, some not; some extensive, some quite short–are also available from national organizations concerned with lesbigay issues. For example, Parents, Families, and Friends of Lesbians and Gays (PFLAG) sells several printed lists,[24] as does the Library Information Clearinghouse of the American Library Association's Gay, Lesbian, and Bisexual Task Force.[25]

Internet sites with helpful lists are abundant. Many of these can be found at "Library Q" (http://carbon.cudenver.edu/public/library/libq/), a site specifically designed to aid libraries dealing with lesbigay library issues and projects. (The bibliographies are located at http://carbon.cuden ver.edu/public/library/libq/books.html#bibs). "Gay, Lesbian, Bisexual, and Transgender Materials: Resources for Librarians" (http://wever.u. washington.edu/~keb/wla/toc.htm), developed by a group of library students, is another useful Web site for bibliographies.

A small sampling of the wide variety of special-topic lesbigay bibliographies and booklists available elsewhere on the Internet includes:

- "Books on Coming Out," compiled by the Human Rights Campaign's National Coming Out Project (http://www.hrcusa.org/who what/whatwedo/ncop/resource/books/html). A similar list is the "Coming Out Reading List," compiled by the lesbigay student group at Indiana University (http//www.indiana.edu/~iu_glb/comingout. reading.list.html).
- "Lesbians, Bisexuals, and Gay Men in the Workplace," compiled by Ray Anne Lockard (http://afalib.uflib.ufl.edu/arlis/publications/gay swork.html).

- "Gay and Lesbian Drama Reading List," compiled by the librarians of the Literature and Languages Division at the Chicago Public Library's Harold Washington Library Center (http://cpl.lib.uic.edu/001hwlc/litlists/gayplays.html).
- "Jewish GLBT-Related Novels," compiled by Johnny Abush of the Jewish GLBT Archives (http://www.magic.ca/~faygelah/JGLBT.Novels.A-N.html and http://www.magic.ca/~faygelah/JGLBT.Novels.OZ.html).
- "Gay and Lesbian Characters and Themes in Children's Books," compiled by Wendy E. Betts (http://www.armory.com/~web/gaybooks.html).
- "Lesbian Studies," compiled by Joan Ariel for the Collection Development and Bibliography Committee of the Association of College and Research Libraries' Women Studies Section (http://www.library.wisc.edu/libraries/WomensStudies/core/crlesb.htm).

Internet search engines created specifically for retrieving lesbigay Internet sites include: "Rainbow Query" (http://www.glweb.com/RainbowQuery/Index.html) and "Lesbian Links" (http://www.lesbian.org/lesbian/). For these two search engines, use the terms *bibliography, bibliographies, booklist, book list, reading list,* etc., to retrieve the relevant information. Both Rainbow Query and Lesbian Links are actually indexes as well as search engines; the former has over 200 categories to choose from. For all-purpose Internet search engines such as Altavista, WebCrawler, Lycos, Excite, Hotbot, and so on, use these same keywords plus the terms *lesbian, gay, bisexual* and their plural (or truncated) forms.

Bundled along with the good news about the wealth of resources available to selectors on the Internet is the stubborn fact that librarians must use Internet sources critically. For various reasons, an Internet site can abruptly change, disappear, or be abandoned by its creators. Because most sites are the result of the effort of a single individual, few of them will be maintained indefinitely and with the thoroughness librarians expect from conventionally published sources. Although some Internet sites are as authoritative, well-organized, current, accurate, and complete as any conventionally published source, others can be more disappointing in one or more of these respects. This is as true for lesbigay-related Internet sites as for those on any other subject.

IDENTIFYING BESTSELLING LESBIGAY BOOKS

Since smaller libraries will be forced by budget constraints to limit their lesbigay purchases strictly to the most popular materials written for nonspecialist readers, locating a regularly assembled list of such bestsellers is an essential tool for many library selectors. Lists of bestselling lesbigay books are available from a variety of sources:

- Magazines catering to lesbigay readers such as *Curve* (formerly *Deneuve), The Advocate,* and *Lambda Book Report* publish bestseller lists. If your library subscribes to these periodicals, you should be able to conveniently monitor their lists.
- *Feminist Bookstore News* includes composite lists of bestselling titles at gay, lesbian, and feminist bookstores throughout the United States and Canada.
- An OCLC and/or RLIN search can tell you how many other libraries (or, if it matters, which libraries) have already purchased a particular title. Finding multiple holdings of a particular title in a union catalog (these or others) is one way–especially for a selector new to lesbigay subject matter–to gauge expected demand for that title.
- Bestseller lists are often available on the World Wide Web pages maintained by the larger lesbian and gay bookstores.[26]
- To obtain information about *local* lesbigay bestsellers, you could make periodic visits to the bookseller in your area specializing in (or at least carrying a large stock of) books for lesbians and/or gay men. More efficient, perhaps, would be making an arrangement with the owner of such a store to mail you a copy of the store's newsletter, which will most likely contain a list of bestsellers.

IDENTIFYING AWARD-WINNING LESBIGAY BOOKS AND AUTHORS

Many librarians prefer to purchase titles judged to be extraordinarily well-written or otherwise important regardless of how well they fare in the retail marketplace. Although the vagaries surrounding award-giving are almost as extensive as the vagaries surrounding "bestsellerdom," literary awards do indicate a perception of perceived importance relative to other titles or authors. Unlike the award-winning titles of other types of books, many award-winning books by lesbians and gay men are still in print.

Three sets of national awards for outstanding lesbigay books or authors are given annually in the United States:

- The oldest awards (established in 1971) are the Gay/Lesbian/Bisexual Book Awards. An award for nonfiction and another for literature are announced each winter by the American Library Association. A list of the current and past winners of these awards is available from the Clearinghouse of the ALA's Gay & Lesbian Task Force and at various Internet sites.[27]

- A more recently-established (1989) but much larger set of annual awards, the "Lammys," are announced each year in conjunction with the convention of the American Booksellers Association. Currently, awards are presented to books in 20 categories. A comprehensive printed list of these award-winning titles is available from the Lambda Literary Foundation [28] and you can also find the list on the Internet.[29]

- Since 1992, The Publishing Triangle has announced four literary awards annually: the year's best fiction by a gay writer, the year's best fiction by a lesbian, the year's best AIDS writing, and a lifetime achievement award.[30]

For selectors who prefer to collect award-winning *authors*' works rather than limiting library purchases to award-winning *titles*, a list-in-progress entitled "Award-Winning Gay and Lesbian Authors" is posted on the Internet at http:carbon.cudenver.edu/public/library/libq/authors.html. Each author entry lists the author's national awards and prizes, specifying titles when awards were given for particular works.

FINDING REVIEWS

Reviews of lesbigay titles appear routinely in the major reviewing journals, with *Library Journal* and *Publishers Weekly* currently publishing more of them per year than the others. The reviews in these two journals, and the reviews from hundreds of other general-audience and specialized magazines and journals, are listed in *Book Review Index (BRI)*.[31] The most efficient means of monitoring reviews of recently-published lesbigay books, however, is to subscribe to one or more journals dedicated to providing this service. Unfortunately, many of these lesbigay review journals are not indexed in *BRI*. Equally unfortunately, most of the journals most librarians rely upon for book reviews are not the journals that publish the most reviews of lesbigay books.[32] This makes it very important that individual libraries subscribe to one or more of these specialized review journals. Those journals are:

- *Lambda Book Review.* Established in 1987 and now published monthly, each issue features 10 to 20 full-length reviews followed by a slightly greater number of shorter reviews. Each issue also includes a list of current bestsellers. Subscriptions are $29.95 per year. Address: P.O. Box 73910, Washington, DC 20056.

- *Harvard Gay and Lesbian Review: A Quarterly Journal of Arts, Letters, and Sciences.* Established in 1994, each issue includes about two dozen full-length book reviews, plus about a half-dozen paragraph-length ones. Subscriptions are $20 per year. Address: P.O. Box 180300, Boston, MA 02118.
- *Lesbian Review of Books.* Published quarterly since 1994, each issue features 25 to 30 standard reviews per issue. *LBR's* unique "Forum" feature presents multiple reviews of controversial books and issues, and its "Second Thoughts" features reader-written reviews of previously-reviewed titles. Each issue also includes bibliographic essays on topics of current interest. Subscriptions are $12 per year. Address: P.O. Box 6369, Altadena, CA 91003.

A final publication useful to library selectors of lesbigay materials is the *Lavender Salon Reader: A Newsletter for Gay and Lesbian Reading Clubs.* Published since 1993, each issue contains several reviews of titles chosen by book discussion groups throughout the country. Subscriptions are $16 for 10 issues per year; the address is The Lavender Salon Press, 1474 Home Avenue, Menasha, WI 54952. A companion Web site, Lavender Salon Reader Online (http://www.athenet.net/~lavsalon), publishes the book reviews after a six-month delay.

If your library subscribes to any lesbigay magazines–and it should be subscribing to at least a few of them–you can also conveniently monitor their book reviews for purchase ideas.

Book Reviews on the Internet for Lesbigay Titles

A major Internet site for lesbigay book reviews is the International Gay & Lesbian Review (http://www.usc.edu/Library/oneigla/onepress/index.html). Available only in electronic form since it began publication in May 1997, fewer than 100 reviews are currently available so far, but more are being added. The core group of reviewers is composed of faculty, students, and other scholars affiliated with the ONE Institute's Center for Advanced Studies at the University of Southern California. The reviews are searchable by author and title, although keyword searching will eventually be possible as well.

Most other Internet review sites for lesbigay titles take a rather casual–or commercial–approach to reviewing books, but they can still be useful to the library selector. Examples are:

- Women's Books Online (http://www.cybergrrl.com/review/), containing a substantial number of reviews of lesbian books.
- HERE (http://www.users.interport.net/~seantg/), Sean Gallagher's personal reviews of gay fiction, nonfiction, and anthologies.
- Gay Lit Now (http://www.geocities.com/WestHollywood/5434/index. html), whose reviews are written by the self-confessed "relatively well-read" amateur Tim Donahue.

Many lesbigay bookstores also review new releases on their Web pages. Examples are: A Different Light in San Francisco (http://www.adlbooks.com/ shelves.html), Full Circle Books in Albuquerque (http://kumo.swap. com//fab/bookrevt.html), and Sisterspirit Bookstore and Coffeehouse (http://www.elf.net/sisterspirit/books.html).

NoveList

A unique and powerful electronic tool available to selectors of lesbigay *fiction*, including fiction for adults, young adults, and children, is *NoveList*, a database available on CD-ROM (often networked on library terminals) and on the Internet. It is produced by CARL Corporation and was created in 1994 as a machine-based, "self-service" reader's advisory service. This cleverly-constructed, user-friendly, and rapidly growing database contains (among other things) subject headings and either plot summaries or *Booklist* reviews for over 20,000 novels, including many written by and for lesbian and gay readers. NoveList is cross-indexed and searchable in many ways, including by subject, author, title, and keywords (include types of characters, time periods, and locales). NoveList uses Hennepin County Library's extensive and gratifyingly specific, natural-language subject headings for fiction (e.g., "gay professional baseball players").[33]

FINDING OUT-OF-PRINT BOOKS

Although lesbigay materials tend to stay in print longer than books on many other subjects, nothing stays in print indefinitely, including many important titles. The longstanding and widespread neglect in collecting lesbigay materials in most libraries means that, for this subject area—and especially in academic libraries—selectors will need to devote some attention to obtaining out-of-print (OP) titles. OP selection in this area is as time-consuming as it is for any area.[34] Selectors of lesbigay materials should also remember to periodically poll the larger lesbigay bookstores when searching for OP lesbigay titles, as all of these stores sell used copies of both hardbound and paperback OP books. Be sure to insist in your "titles needed" letters that the physical condition of any used copies offered for sale needs to be suitable for adding to a library collection.

CREATING SHELFLISTS AND CONDUCTING INVENTORIES

Although undeniably labor-intensive, creating a shelflist of lesbigay titles in your collection (or at least the part of the collection you select for) can be extremely useful in various ways. The multidisciplinary nature of many lesbian and gay books usually results in those books being widely separated on the shelves of libraries. This dispersal makes a shelflist almost mandatory if a selector intends to be systematic about filling gaps and monitoring which missing titles need replacing. Periodic inventories based on your shelflist, along with examinations of any routinely published reports of unreturned books generated by your circulation system, are virtually the only way to regularly and empirically gauge the actual availability of the lesbigay materials in your collection, as opposed to merely counting how many titles you or others have *purchased* at one time or another. Lesbigay books–like books about car repair, UFOs, and a host of otherwise unrelated topics–tend (for different reasons) to disappear from libraries more often than books on most other subjects. It is particularly important for selectors of lesbigay books to find ways to monitor the *continued availability* of their purchases rather than considering their work completed after they have submitted their orders.

Be careful when assembling your shelflist to make sure you have checked your catalog for all the relevant subject headings and/or call numbers. Because lesbigay books have been cataloged so differently over the years, it is easy to miss entire groups of titles classified under obsolete headings.

How often you conduct an inventory should probably depend on the size of your collection. If your library's collection is a very large one, you might consider enlisting a colleague or a library volunteer to help you, although the information gleaned from personally inspecting your collection–as opposed to reviewing data collected by someone else, or by relying on bibliographic records instead of the collection itself–is invaluable.

If you eventually move on to other selection responsibilities, be sure to explain your shelflist and any past inventories based on it to the person taking over your duties: comparing data from inventories conducted several years apart will reveal patterns relevant to collection maintenance and development.

TOPICS TO COVER

The range of reading interests among lesbian and gay library users is extremely broad. Selectors in this subject area should be sure to include titles that reflect these varied interests rather than unintentionally limiting their selections to only a few of these interests. A library collection that adequately addresses the concerns and interests of lesbian and gay library users will include books on the following subjects (listed here in alphabetical order as they are equally important):

- biography
- coming out
- health issues
- history and politics
- legal and financial issues
- literature
- relationships (including parenting)
- religion and spirituality
- sex instruction
- travel (U.S. and international)
- visual and performing arts

"Literature," for lesbian and gay readers like other kinds of readers, includes poetry and drama as well as novels and short story collections and anthologies.

A CHECKLIST FOR SELECTORS

Questions and reminders are also valuable items in a selector's "toolkit." For the selector of lesbigay library materials, the most crucial questions are:

- Are you giving equal attention (and devoting equal resources) to purchasing for lesbians and gay men? If not, do you have a logical reason for not doing so?
- Are you making efforts to identify books written by or for people of color?
- Are you ordering books for the people in all age groups who use your library? If you select materials for only one age group, have you spoken to selectors for other age groups about their selection plans or practices regarding lesbigay materials?

• Are you purchasing materials published in other English-language-speaking countries, especially from publishers in Canada, the United Kingdom, Australia, and New Zealand? Important gay and lesbian titles are consistently published in these countries.

LESBIGAY REFERENCE BOOKS

Libraries that cannot afford to maintain an adequate collection of lesbigay circulating monographs should at least provide lesbigay materials that can be used inside the library. Although the number of lesbigay reference works is steadily growing, there are a few essential ones that should be in the collections of all but the tiniest of libraries.[35]

Although it isn't an exhaustive list, *American Reference Book Annual (ARBA)*[36] often includes lesbigay reference titles you may have missed in monitoring a previous year's worth of standard and specialized review publications. Check *ARBA*'s title index under the words *Gay* and *Lesbian*—unfortunately, there is no subject index to search.

A near-comprehensive Internet resource describing lesbigay reference books is compiled by Al Fritz of the University of Washington Libraries: "Gays and Lesbians: An Annotated Guide to Reference and Bibliographical Works" (http://weber.u.washington.edu/~refquest/gay.html). Consisting of over a hundred citations, each accompanied by an evaluative annotation, this list covers a variety of topics that includes politics, law, history, literature, language, publishing resources, special collections in libraries, and more.

In addition to helping meet the information needs of your library's gay and lesbian users, maintaining an adequate collection of lesbigay reference books will help library selectors with their selection duties, as these sources invariably contain excellent book lists.

AN IMPORTANT CHALLENGE

The remarkable recent growth in the number of books and audiovisual materials produced for gay, lesbian, and bisexual readers, viewers, and listeners in this country—especially the growth in the number of lesbigay books produced by an ever-growing number of smaller publishers—is taking place at the same time that funds at many libraries for purchasing library materials of any kind (except perhaps computer-based information resources) has been steadily decreasing. The convergence of these two trends makes it even more important than ever that library selectors be judicious and efficient in their purchases of every type of material, including those produced by and for lesbians and gay men. Selectors can "work smarter, not harder" by becoming familiar with the wide assortment of selection tools, including an increasing number of tools on the Internet, now available for identifying these materials. No matter what kind of library you work for, or how much or little money you have to spend, your numerous gay and lesbian library users depend on your conscientious effort to take into account their information needs and leisure reading interests as you go about your work.

RECOMMENDED READING FOR NOVICE LESBIGAY BOOK SELECTORS

Cruikshank, Margaret. *The Gay & Lesbian Liberation Movement* (Routledge, Chapman, & Hall, 1992), pp. 107-115.

Gough, Cal, and Greenblatt, Ellen (eds.). *Gay and Lesbian Library Service* (McFarland, 1990).

Kraus, Joseph R. "Book Information and Reviews on the Web," *Information Outlook*, September 1997, pp. 9-10.

Ammons, Elizabeth, and others (eds.) *Oxford Companion to Women's Writing in the United States* (Oxford University Press, 1995). See the articles on Queer Theory, Lesbian Publishing Outlets, Lesbian Pulp Fiction, Lesbian Writing, plus entries on individual authors (Adrienne Rich, e.g.).

Thomsen, Elizabeth. *Reference and Collection Development on the Internet.* (How-to-Do-It Manuals for Librarians, Number 66) Neal Schuman Publishers, 1996.

REFERENCES

1. Eric Bryant ("Pride and Prejudice," *Library Journal*, June 15, 1995, 37-39) found that, of a group of 250 public and college libraries, 50% had fewer than 30 books with lesbigay themes or characters, 26% had fewer than 150 such books, and 13% had fewer than 500 such books. While 10% of the libraries polled had collected at least 500 books with lesbigay themes or characters, a greater number, 14%, had no such books at all.

2. James H. Sweetland and Peter G. Christensen ("Gay Lesbian and Bisexual Titles: Their Treatment in the Review Media and Their Selection by Libraries,"

Collection Building (1995) 14(2): 32-41) found that lesbigay titles are collected less often than non-lesbigay titles regardless of how often or favorably they are reviewed.

3. Cal Gough and Ellen Greenblatt, "Services to Gay and Lesbian Patrons: Examining the Myths," *Library Journal* (January 1992): 59-63.

4. This article's focus is selecting materials of interest to library users who are *lesbians* or *gay men*. In this article we refer to these materials as "lesbigay" materials. Tools for selecting materials of interest to *bisexual* or *transgendered* library users (and their families, friends, and acquaintances—and other constituencies for these materials) deserve separate treatment, although to some extent the information provided will result in identification of some of those materials.

5. A discussion of the larger context of lesbigay collection development, including the unique challenges and constraints faced by selectors of lesbigay materials, can be found in the authors' anthology *Gay and Lesbian Library Service* (McFarland, 1990).

6. You need not be a lesbian or gay man yourself to be an effective and efficient selector of lesbigay materials.

7. Lesbigay materials are available in all formats (video, audio, microform, CD-ROM, and periodicals). The fact that the scope of this article is limited to describing tools for selecting lesbigay *books* should not be construed to mean that librarians should not collect lesbigay materials in other formats, *especially periodicals*. Librarians with an interest in improving their collections of lesbigay periodicals will benefit from reading Thomas Kilpatrick's "Critical Look at the Availability of Gay and Lesbian Periodical Literature in Libraries and Standard Indexing Sources" (*Serials Review*, Winter 1997, 71-81). As Kirkpatrick mentions in his article, the primary selection tool for lesbigay periodicals is the group of annotations in *Magazines for Libraries* (Bowker). The 1995 edition describes the content and intended audience for some 90 items suitable for libraries.

8. See, for example, Bob Summer, "Gay and Lesbian Publishing: The Paradox of Success," *Publishers Weekly* (June 7, 1993): 36-40 and Juana Ponce de Leon, "Reflections on a Growing Market," *Publishers Weekly* (December 8, 1989): 24.

9. Beginning in January 1998, *BIP Plus* will also include video and audio titles as well as books. For more information on Books in Print products, contact Reed/Elsevier or check the Web site at http://www.bowker.com/epcatalog/home/edbip/html.

10. Mainstream commercial and academic publishers currently producing several lesbigay titles each season include: Bantam, Cassell Academic, Columbia University, Dell, Doubleday, Duke University, Faber & Faber, The Feminist Press at the City University of New York, Gale Research (including its St. James Press and Visible Ink imprints), Garland, Greenwood, HarperCollins, The Haworth Press, Inc., Indiana University, New York University, Penguin USA (especially its Dutton, Plume, and Viking imprints), Pocket Books, Princeton University, Random House (especially Ballantine and Knopf), Routledge, Simon & Schuster, and St. Martin's (including its Stonewall Inn imprint). Lesbian- or gay-owned publish-

ers include: Alyson Publications, Firebrand Books, Cleis Press, GLB Publishers, GMP Publishers, Naiad Press, New Victoria Publishers, Pres Gang Publishers, Seal Press, Sister Vision Press, and Spinsters Ink.

11. Vendors with lesbian- or gay-themed catalogs include:

- Bookazine, 75 Hook Road, Bayonne, NJ 07002. Phone: (800) 221-8112. E-mail: EdwardE8@aol.com. URL: http://www.bookazine.com.

- Bookpeople, 7900 Edgewater Drive, Oakland, CA 94621. Phone: (510) 632-4700. E-mail: custserv@bponline.com. URL: http://www.bponline.com.

- Koen Book Distributors, 10 Twosome Drive, Box 600, Moorestown, NJ 08057. Phone: (800) 257-8481. E-mail: kbd@koen.com. URL: http://www.koen.com.

- LPC Group, 1436 West Randolph Street, Chicago, IL 60607. Phone: (800) 621-4249 or (800) 626-4330. E-mail: lm@lbbc.lb.com. URL: http://www.lb.com/lpc.

12. Alamo Square Press, P.O. Box 14543, San Francisco, CA 94114. Phone: (415) 863-7410.

13. Women's Presses Library Project, c/o Mev Miller, Project Coordinator, 1483 Laurel Avenue, St. Paul, MN 55104. Phone: (612) 646-0097. E-mail: wplp@winternet.com. URL: http://carbon.cudenver.edu/public/library/library/libq/wplp.html.

14. The Publishing Triangle, P.O. Box 114, Prince Street Station, New York, NY 10012.

15. GLBTF Clearinghouse, c/o ALA Office of Outreach Services, 50 East Huron Street, Chicago, IL 60611. An electronic order form for Clearinghouse publications is available on the Internet (http://www-lib.usc.edu/~trimmer/ala_form.html).

16. See, for example, Lars Eighner's "Your Local Gay Bookstore" (http://www.io.com/~eighner/stores.html) or "Lesbian and Gay Bookstore Index" (http://www.www.qrd.ord/QRD/www/media./print/bookstores/glbwnets.html) as well as the "Feminist Bookstores Index" (http://www.igc.apc.org/women/bookstores/widenets.html).

17. *Feminist Bookstore News*, P.O. Box 882554, San Francisco, CA 94188. E-mail: FBN@FemBkNews.com.

18. For more information about OCLC and WorldCat, contact OCLC at 6565 Frantz Road, Dublin, OH 43017. Phone: (614) 764-6000. E-mail: oclc@oclc.org. URL: http://www.oclc.org/oclc/address/contac.htm.

19. For more information about RLIN, contact The Research Library Group, 1200 Villa Street, Mountain View, CA 94041. Phone: (800) 537-RLIN. E-mail: bl.ric@rlg.org. URL: http://lyra.rlg.org.

20. For more information about CARL Uncover Books-in-Reveal, contact Uncover by phone at (303) 758-3030, by e-mail at uncover@carl.org, or via CARL's web page at http://uncweb.carl.org/reveal/revbooks.html.

21. GAY-LIBN is dedicated to the concerns and interests of gay, lesbian, and bisexual library workers and friends. As such, issues discussed may include politi-

cal action, AIDS education, outreach programs, social programs, notices of what other groups, individuals, and librarians are doing, and general library issues. To subscribe to GAY-LIBN, send the following message to listproc@usc.edu: subscribe gay-libn YourFirstName YourLastName. To post messages to the list, send them to gaylibn@usc.edu. For more information, contact list owner Keith Trimmer (trimmer@calvin.usc.edu).

22. LEZBRIAN is a forum for discussing professional issues of interest to lesbian and bisexual women library workers. To join the list and receive mailings from LEZBRIAN, send the following message to listserv@listserv.acsu.buffalo. edu: subscribe lezbrian YourFirstName YourLastName. To post messages to the list, send them to lezbrian@listserv.acsu.buffalo.edu. Only subscribers may post to the list. For more information, contact list owners Jerilyn Veldof (jveldof @bird.library.arizona.edu) or Ellen Greenblatt (egreenbl@carbon.cudenver.edu) or visit the Web page at http://www.library.arizona.edu/users/jveldof/lezbrian/ lezbrian.html.

23. A few recent attempts include Wayne R. Dynes, *Homosexuality: A Research Guide* (New York: Garland Publishing, 1987) and Margaret Gillon, *Lesbians in Print: A Bibliography of 1,500 Books with Synopses* (Irvine, CA: Bluestocking Books, 1995). Until mid-September 1997 when time constraints forced her to discontinue doing so, Gillon updated her publication on the World Wide Web at http://home.earthlink.net/~griffgill/.

24. PFLAG, 1101 14th Street, NW, Suite 1030, Washington, DC 20005. Phone: (202) 638-4200. E-mail: info@pflag.org. URL: http://www.pflag.org/.

25. An example of the information available from the Task Force is its unannotated but quite comprehensive list, updated twice a year by librarian Don Bell, of well over 300 book-length items relating to the spiritual lives of lesbians and gay men.

26. See, for example, the pages maintained by A Brother's Touch in Minneapolis (http://www.loringwebservices.com/brotherstouch/books/bestsellers.html); A Different Light in San Francisco (http://www.adlbooks.com/sfb.html); Glad Day Bookshop in Boston (http://web0.tiac.net/users/gladday/!html/wnlt.htm); and The Open Book in Sacramento (http://www.openbookltd.com/top.HTM).

27. To find award information on the Web, see "Library Q: Award Winning Books" (http://carbon.cudenver.edu/public/library/libq/books.html/#award). Information about the ALA awards themselves, see http://www-lib.usc.edu/~trim mer/ala_book.html.

28. Lambda Literary Foundation, c/o Lambda Rising, Inc., 1625 Connecticut Avenue, NW, Washington, DC 20009. Phone: (202) 462-7924. E-mail: LBRO JimM@aol.com.

29. A list of Lambda Literary Award winners can be found at http://www. amazon.com/. (Choose "Award Winners" and then "Lambda Literary Awards.")

30. See Note 14 for contact information.

31. Neil E. Walker and Beverly Baer, eds., *Book Review Index* (Detroit: Gale Research, published quarterly and cumulated annually).

32. See James H. Sweetland and Peter G. Christensen, "Gay Lesbian and Bisexual Titles: Their Treatment in the F view Media and Their Selection by Libraries," *Collection Building* (1995) 14(2): 32-41.

33. Information on NoveList is available from CARL Corporation, 3801 East Florida Avenue, Suite 300, Denver, CO 80210. Phone: (888) 439-2275. E-mail: novelist@carl.org. URL: http://www.carl.org/novelist.

34. Books Bohemian is the largest OP dealer in lesbigay books in the United States and you should definitely put your name on the mailing list for its catalogs. Address: 2121 West 9th Street, Los Angeles, CA 90006; P.O. Box 17218, Los Angeles, CA 90017. Phone: (213) 385-6761. Another dealer specializing in OP lesbigay books is Everglades Book Company, P.O. Box 2425, Bonita Springs, FL 34133. Phone: (941) 353-4314. E-mail: evergladesbookcompany@msn.com. URL: http://www.evergladesbookcompany.com.y

35. In addition to the works cited in Note 21, the steadily-growing list of essential lesbigay reference works includes:

- Michael J. Tyrkus, ed., *Gay and Lesbian Biography* (Detroit: St. James Press, 1997).

- Randy P. Conner, David Hatfield Sparks, and Mariya Sparks, *Cassell's Encyclopedia of Queer Myth, Symbol, and Spirit: Gay, Lesbian, Bisexual, and Transgender Lore* (London: Cassell, 1997).

- Hayden Curry, *A Legal Guide for Lesbian and Gay Couples*, 9th national ed. (Berkeley: Nolo Press, 1996).

- Raymond Curry, *Images in the Dark: An Encyclopedia of Gay and Lesbian Film and Video* (Philadelphia: TLA Publications, 1996).

- National Museum & Archives of Lesbian and Gay History, *The Gay Almanac* (New York: Berkeley Books, 1996).

- National Museum & Archives of Lesbian and Gay History, *The Lesbian Almanac* (New York: Berkeley Books, 1996).

- William Stewart, *Cassell's Queer Companion: A Dictionary of Lesbian and Gay Life and Culture* (London: Cassell, 1995).

- Claude J. Summers, ed., *The Gay and Lesbian Literary Heritage* (New York: Henry Holt, 1995).

- Eric Marcus, *Is It a Choice? Answers to 300 of the Most Frequently Asked Questions About Gays and Lesbians* (San Francisco: HarperSanFrancisco, 1993).

- Emmanuel S. Nelson, ed., *Contemporary Gay American Novelists: A Bio-Bibliographical Critical Sourcebook* (Westport, CT: Greenwood Press, 1993).

- Wayne R. Dynes, ed., *Encyclopedia of Homosexuality* (New York: Garland Publishing, 1990).

36. Bohdan S. Wynar, ed., *American Reference Books Annual* (Littleton, CO: Libraries Unlimited, annual).

Multicultural Children's Literature Selection and Evaluation: Incorporating the World Wide Web

Dana Watson

SUMMARY. Children need access to literature representing their own culture, that of their community, and cultures beyond their immediate experience. Selecting quality multicultural children's literature involves identifying and evaluating potential materials, with special consideration of cultural accuracy and authenticity. Web based resources can supplement standard selection tools and uniquely contribute to this process. Review sources, bibliographies, and guides located on the world wide web suggest quality multicultural titles for children and provide guidance for selectors in choosing authentic materials. This article lists useful web sites for selectors of multicultural children's literature. *[Article copies available for a fee from The Haworth Document Delivery Service: 1-800-342-9678. E-mail address: getinfo@haworthpressinc.com]*

INTRODUCTION

Today's youth services librarians utilize the world wide web to develop quality multicultural children's literature collections. Web resources provide access to information not available or not easily accessible in the

Dana Watson is Assistant Professor, School of Library and Information Science, 267 Coates Hall, Louisiana State University, Baton Rouge, LA 70803.

[Haworth co-indexing entry note]: "Multicultural Children's Literature Selection and Evaluation: Incorporating the World Wide Web." Watson, Dana. Co-published simultaneously in *The Acquisitions Librarian* (The Haworth Press, Inc.) No. 20, 1998, pp. 171-183; and: *Public Library Collection Development in the Information Age* (ed: Annabel K. Stephens) The Haworth Press, Inc., 1998, pp. 171-183. Single or multiple copies of this article are available for a fee from The Haworth Document Delivery Service [1-800-342-9678, 9:00 a.m. - 5:00 p.m. (EST). E-mail address: getinfo@haworthpressinc.com].

local community. Librarians use web resources in the evaluation and selection process to supplement traditional methods, not to supplant them. It is the intent of this article to review traditional collection development strategies and to suggest how current web sites can be integrated into the identification, evaluation, and selection of multicultural children's literature appropriate for preschoolers through young adults. In addition, a list of web sites useful in the selection and evaluation process of multicultural children's literature will be provided.

Multicultural literature has been defined by Norton as "literature about racial or ethnic minority groups that are culturally and socially different from the white Anglo-Saxon majority in the United States, whose largely middle-class values and customs are most represented in American literature."[1] Yokota describes multicultural literature as that which "represents any distinct cultural group through accurate portrayal and rich detail."[2] Often the term is limited to materials by or about people of color—those ethnic and racial groups that comprise much of the United States today: African Americans, Asian Americans, Hispanics, and Native Americans. A more inclusive definition encompasses any distinct cultural group not in mainstream society, such as people of a particular age, gender, religion, sexual orientation, physical ability or class. This paper's discussion will address a broad range of resources, attempting to be as inclusive as possible.

RATIONALE

Today, according to the census bureau, almost one in 10 U.S. residents was born in another country. Leading sources of newcomers include Mexico, the Philippines, China, Cuba, and India. Of this foreign born population, almost half is Hispanic, one-fifth is Asian, and one-twelfth is black. If this trend continues, by the middle of the next century the U.S. will be a fully racially mixed nation.[3] Our young people of today need to be prepared for the global society they will inhabit as adults and to realize people throughout the world are more alike than different. Multicultural children's literature presents children with opportunities to develop understandings about other people and cultures. These insights can influence decisions about how to live in this culturally pluralistic world and how to relate to those whose cultural backgrounds may differ from one's own.

There are advantages for children to read literature which emanates from both inside and outside their own cultural heritage. Reading about one's own culture leads to insights about heritage and can enhance pride and self-concept. Reading about other cultures can lead to increased knowledge of other people and allow readers to vicariously experience another culture. In building our library collections, we want to allow children both of these opportunities. First, we want to reflect the diversity of our own communities. This includes both visible and less visible minority groups. Secondly, we need to go beyond our own borders and ensure that global diversity is represented in the literature available for our young people. Above all, we want to make sure what we do provide children of our communities is authentic and accurate.

EVALUATING MULTICULTURAL LITERATURE

Many children's books produced over the years have depicted cultural groups negatively, inaccurately, as objects of curiosity, or simply ignored them. If the story did not take place in a white, Protestant, middle class, economically advantaged, two-parent family, it generally focused on non-Caucasians with a problem, took place in an urban setting, or described specific cultural practices of a group. Today, fortunately, this situation is improving but there is still reason to suggest judicious use and constant evaluation.

Evaluation of multicultural children's literature demands application of the same criteria as any other literature being considered for acquisition. Qualities such as a well-written text, appropriate setting, point of view, characterization, plot, theme, and style are important considerations. The engagement of the reader with story is of primary importance. Most selectors are comfortable judging strengths and weaknesses in these traditional evaluative arenas. Selectors of multicultural children's literature, however, must also pay particular attention to the cultural accuracy and authenticity of these materials. Many selectors have little experience and/or knowledge of other cultures and find it difficult to make informed decisions about accuracy and authenticity. Certainly no one individual is expert on the many cultures represented in our society. There are, fortunately, several approaches available for librarians to ensure appropriate choices.

Selectors evaluate materials (1) through personal examination, (2) by accessing published reviews, and (3) by seeking out opinions of experts. Both traditional selection tools and resources on the world wide web support these methods. Librarians selecting children's literature, including multicultural children's literature, follow one or more of these evaluation processes. In fact, library policies often require these procedures be employed before purchasing children's materials.[4]

Personal Examination

When materials are readily accessible, personal examination can allow a selector to individually evaluate potential multicultural children's resources in terms of community needs, quality of the literature, and cultural representation. Evaluation of cultural accuracy and authenticity requires, however, a degree of cultural awareness that may only evolve with time and commitment.

Individuals can develop personal knowledge about a culture by reading a wide variety of quality literature representative of that culture. For example, African American children's authors Virginia Hamilton, Walter Dean Myers, and Mildred Taylor transmit experiences of the culture through events, insights and perspectives in the lives of their characters. Children's literature selectors should seek out and read notable examples from a variety of cultures. Reading adult literature is also valuable to gain understandings of the beliefs, values, and contributions of a group of people. Bibliographies such as Lyn Miller-Lachmann's *Our Family, Our Friends, Our World*[5] and *Global Voices, Global Visions*[6] list recommended authors and titles of children's and adult materials, respectively, and can provide entrance into this world of literature. Other recommended titles can be located on web sites representing particular groups such as Native Americans, African Americans, Latino/as, etc. Reading a variety of accepted texts can develop a depth of experience to bring to the personal examination process and provide background for the application of evaluative criteria.

Evaluation guidelines are particularly useful to weigh the merits of a multicultural book. The Council on Interracial Books for Children's "Ten Quick Ways to Analyze Children's Books for Sexism and Racism" suggests looking at the illustrations, story line, lifestyles, relationships, heroes, copyright date and watching for loaded words as well as considering the effects on a child's self-image. The authors' perspectives and authors' or illustrators' backgrounds can also be considerations.[7] Evaluation criteria often take the form of questions:

1. Are the characters portrayed as individuals instead of as representatives of a group?
2. Does the book transcend stereotypes?
3. Does the book portray physical diversity?
4. Will children be able to recognize the characters in the text and illustrations?
5. Is the culture accurately portrayed?

6. Are social issues and problems depicted frankly, accurately, and without oversimplification?
7. Do nonwhite characters solve their problems without intervention by whites?
8. Are nonwhite characters shown as equals of white characters?
9. Does the author avoid glamorization or glorifying nonwhite characters?
10. Is the setting authentic?
11. Are the factual and historical details accurate?
12. Does the author accurately describe contemporary settings?
13. Does the book rectify historical distortions or omissions?
14. Does dialect have a legitimate purpose and does it ring true?
15. Does the author avoid offensive or degrading vocabulary?
16. Are the illustrations authentic and nonstereotypical?
17. Does the book reflect an awareness of the changing status of females?[8]

Similar criteria exist to guide authors in their writing of multicultural works. These guidelines list qualities librarians also value (strong three-dimensional characters, cultural specificity, etc.) and provide additional points for selectors to consider. One example, recommended components for authentic multicultural literature dealing with Afrocentric themes, has been compiled by small press publisher Just Us Books and is available at the Multicultural Publishing and Education Council web site.

Published Reviews

Librarians consult published reviews to learn about recently published materials and to determine the quality of those resources. Selectors of children's materials examine review journals such as *Booklist, The Bulletin of the Center for Children's Books, The Horn Book Magazine, Kirkus, School Library Journal,* and *VOYA.* Many, though certainly not all, newly published, quality multicultural books can be identified through these journals. Specialized journals such as *Multicultural Review* offer evaluative reviews specifically related to multicultural literature while subject specific journals *(Language Arts, Reading Teacher)* also publish pertinent reviews. Today, many of these journals provide access to their reviews through web sites. Depending on the journal, web site information may include complete review coverage of back issue(s), selected reviews, tables of contents, cumulated indexes (often not yet available in their print counterpart), subject access, and combinations of these features. Continual monitoring of a number of review journals allows selectors to be aware of not only newly available multicultural materials but also their quality as established by professional or volunteer reviewers.

Opinions of Experts

Seeking opinions of experts is another way to gain insight about the accuracy and authenticity of multicultural literature. Asking members of a culture to review material locally is one way to accomplish this. Another is to read books and articles which discuss the merits of particular titles. These sources often incorporate authors' comments and discuss aspects of authenticity through bibliographic essays. *Through Indian Eyes: The Native Experience in Children's Books,*[9] and *Shadow and Substance,*[10] for example, are well known for evaluating specific titles for authenticity. Many of the examples discussed in such resources provide insights useful when evaluating similar works.

Opinions of experts from particular cultures can also be accessed through web sites of specific groups. For example, Native American groups have several sites in which discussions of authenticity in literature can be located. Indeed, many groups and organizations have their own small presses which produce literature representative of their culture. Often this material is not covered in review journals. The web, in this case, functions as both an identification and evaluation vehicle.

RETROSPECTIVE COLLECTION DEVELOPMENT

Typically, librarians seeking quality children's resources to augment particular subject areas consult comprehensive sources such as *Children's Catalog,*[11] *Middle and Junior High School Catalog,*[12] *Senior High School Catalog,*[13] or *Elementary School Library Collection.*[14] For multicultural children's literature specifically, librarians use books like *Against Borders,*[15] *Connecting Cultures,*[16] *The Multicolored Mirror,*[17] *Our Family, Our Friends, Our World,*[18] *Teaching Multicultural Literature in Grades K-8,*[19] *Using Multiethnic Literature in the K-8 Classroom,*[20] or *This Land is Our Land.*[21] Other useful tools for retrospective collection development are periodicals.

Journals regularly publish special bibliographies focusing on specific cultural groups. *Booklist,* for example, publishes bibliographies of materials from a variety of cultures on a regular basis. *Book Links* includes retrospective reviews and bibliographies. These American Library Association (ALA) sponsored journals include cumulated indexes to their contents on their web sites. Web based cumulated indexes like these can streamline the search for reviews of particular titles, authors, or materials related to a certain identified group.

Bibliographies of recommended multicultural children's books are also available on the web. For example, the Cooperative Children's Book Center lists "Twenty-five Multicultural Books Every Child Should Know."[22] Using the traditional print resources in combination with selected bibliographies available on the world wide web can be very useful for building initial collections of multicultural children's literature or supplementing existing ones. Another useful type of bibliography is an award list.

A number of awards are given for children's books that reflect diversity or are international in scope. Titles selected from these lists and included in multicultural children's literature collections can contribute to a global perspective. Several of these awards are presented by organizations affiliated with ALA: The Pura Belpré Award is given biennially to a Latino/Latina writer and illustrator whose work best "portrays, affirms and celebrates the Latino cultural experience in an outstanding work of literature for children and youth."[23] The Mildred L. Batchelder Award is given annually to an American publisher for the most outstanding translated book of the year. To be eligible, the book has to have been originally published in a foreign language and in a foreign country, and subsequently published in the United States. To recognize outstanding books by African-American authors and illustrators, the Coretta Scott King Award is presented annually. Books published in the previous year are selected on the basis of child appeal and sensitivity to the worth and value of all individuals.

Another organization, The Consortium of Latin American Studies Programs (CLASP), presents the annual Américas Award for Children's and Young Adult Literature to recognize a U.S. work, published in the previous year in either Spanish or English, which authentically and engagingly presents the experiences of individuals in Latin America, the Caribbean, or of Latinos in the United States. These books are selected for the quality of their story, cultural authenticity/sensitivity, and potential for classroom use. Information about other award winning books, including international and multinational awards, can be located in print sources like *Children's Books: Awards and Prizes*[24] and on several children's literature related sites on the world wide web. Awards provide an introduction to some of the quality multicultural materials available to our children.

Traditional print selection tools and review journals are invaluable resources when developing or strengthening a multicultural children's literature collection. Web resources are also important collection development tools but, lacking the established authority of many print resources, must be evaluated in terms of their own reliability and credibility.

EVALUATING WEB SITES

A prerequisite to incorporating web sites into the selection and evaluation process is the ability to determine the validity of the sites themselves. Many sites are information rich and are supported by individuals or groups with established authority and expertise. University and government sites often fall into this category. Other sites may be commercial in nature and intent upon selling product. Yet, these sites could still be useful for identifying and confirming the availability of multicultural materials, and perhaps even in evaluation of the literature, although this aspect is more problematical.

Other sites may exist simply because the individuals responsible for constructing them have an interest in the subject. Because anyone can set up a web page, it is critical that each site be evaluated in terms of its own authority and quality. Fortunately there are an increasing number of guidelines available to assist in the evaluation of web resources. Many of these guidelines are available on the web.[25] Concerns about accuracy, authority, and reliability predominate when evaluating web sites but ease of use, arrangement and searching capability also impact ultimate usability.

CONCLUSION

Selectors of multicultural children's literature need to use all available resources to identify and evaluate appropriate publications for their communities. Recommended resources, whether recently published or respected over time, can be identified through standard selection tools and through world wide web resources. Since some of this literature emanates from smaller presses whose publications are not always covered in standard selection tools, web based sites provide an important avenue for the identification and selection of quality literature for children, literature which represents our global society. Additionally, web based sites can assist in the evaluation of cultural accuracy and authenticity of specific texts.

Children deserve access to quality literature which represents the many cultures of today's global community. Our responsibilities as selectors are to know recommended resources among those currently available, to recognize materials which are culturally accurate and authentic, and to provide them for our young people. This melding of expertise and effort assures the best in multicultural children's literature is available for our global citizens of the future.

USEFUL WEB SITES

The following list of world wide web sites reflects the selection and evaluation process and provides access to information about specific cultural groups. Placement of a site within a certain category denotes a strong emphasis of that site, but information relevant to all phases of the selection and evaluation process may be located there. The list is not exhaustive, but rather a sampling of what is available. Many listed sites provide links to additional sites, essentially extending the range of related information. As always, web sites are dynamic organisms and what was available when compiling the list may change in content or location.

How to Find Out What's New: Review Sites

Booklist provides a cumulated index to reviews published in the journal and a list of bibliographies published in the journal in the youth section (including multicultural topics).
http://www.ala.org/booklist/

Bulletin of the Center for Children's Books includes concise summaries and critical evaluations of children's books and Blue Ribbon lists of best books from the previous year (from 1990 on).
http://edfu.lis.uiuc.edu/puboff/bccb/

How to Find Out What's Good: Award Lists

The *Cooperative Children's Book Center* includes the Batchelder, Pura Belpré, and CLASP awards, lists of small presses owned and operated by people of color, and a basic reading list of multicultural books for every child.
http://www.soemadison.wisc.edu/ccbc/

Bibliographies

Book Links has a cumulated index to contents of the journal and a subject access to multicultural bibliographies ("Reading the World"), and annota-

tions of titles.
http://www.ala.org/booklinks

Carol Hurst's Children's Literature site has bibliographies and reviews with teaching suggestions. This site, not necessarily multicultural in focus, does include information on Native American titles.
http://www.carolhurst.com/

Encyclopedia Smithsonian includes a list of publications for children on Native American subjects.
http://www.si.edu/resource/faq/start.htm

LARC Fact Sheet–Multicultural and Ethnic Materials was created by ALA to provide access to multicultural bibliographies printed in *Booklist*. The bibliographies themselves are not listed, but citations to various bibliographies are provided.
http://www.ala.org/library/fact23.html

Multicultural Children's Books by the not-for-profit source, Red & Black Books Collective, provides quality materials often difficult to locate. The brief annotations, with suggested reading levels, are divided by focus: Native heritage, Asian, African, and Latino heritage and general diversity books for children.
http://www.redblack.com/multiki.htm

Notes from the Windowsill (by Wendy Betts) provides children's book reviews and bibliographies (annotated) of best books and special topics, including Jewish culture, multiracial families, and gay and lesbian themes.
http://www.armory.com/~web/notes.html

Guides

The Children's Literature Web Guide includes extensive information on literature for children and young adults. It is one of the best sites available and provides links to bibliographies on multicultural topics.
http://www.ucalgary.ca/~dkbrown/

Education World includes a section on multiculturalism–preparing students for a diverse and global society. Found here are links to multicultural literature, scholarly information, multicultural education, bilingual education and specific information about evaluating multicultural literature.
http://www.education-world.com/whats_new/

An *Instructor* page includes criteria to use in selecting multicultural books, reviews of highly recommended children's books K-8, interviews

and advice with authors representing Native Americans, Latinos, African Americans, Asian Americans and Jewish culture, and related resources.
http://scholastic.com/Instructor/hot/multicultural.htm

Kay Vandergrift maintains a page with information and links to children's literature sites, women's studies, and resources for those who work with children and young people. Related pages provide information about authors and illustrators of children's books, gender and culture.
http://www.scils.rutgers.edu/special/kay/kayhp2.html

The Multicultural Book Review Homepage provides qualitative reviews of K-12 materials. The books are placed on a graded scale, divided into broad classifications (African American, Asian American/Pacific Islander, Jewish, multiple ethnicities, textbooks, etc.) The reviews contain evaluative information and a statement of age/grade suitability.
http://www.isomedia.com/homes/jmele/homepage.html

Multicultural Literature in the Elementary Classroom provides citations from ERIC on selecting and utilizing multicultural children's literature.
http://www.indiana.edu/~eric_rec/ieo/bibs/multicul.html

How to Find Out What's Available: Publisher Sites

Bookwire provides extensive links to review sources, awards, publishers, and library pages related to literature for young readers.
http://WWW.BOOKWIRE.COM/index/Publishing-for-Young-Rdrs.html

The Multicultural Publishing and Education Council is a "national networking and support organization for independent publishers, authors, educators, and librarians fostering authentic multicultural books and materials." It provides information on authenticity of multicultural books, and on multicultural publishers.
http://www.mpec.org/mpec.html

Bookseller Sites

Circle of Friends: Multicultural Books for Children describes books available and allows browsing by age/grade and cultural theme (African-American/Asian-American/Hispanic/Jewish & The Holocaust/Native American/Gay-Lesbian/Children & AIDS/Differently Abled/Multicultural). It provides specific information about selection processes used for its somewhat limited lists of titles.
http://www.cofbooks.com

Shen's Books and Supplies includes children's books representing Asia, Latin America, and Eastern Europe. Provides subject searches, and descriptive (not evaluative) annotations.
http://www.shens.com

How to Find Out More About Other Cultures: Educational Sites

The Multicultural Pavilion at the University of Virginia has as its mission to "provide resources for educators interested in multicultural issues." While the focus is on multicultural education rather than literature, this page lists many areas of interest which can be accessed.
http://curry.edschool.virginia.edu/go/multicultural/

Specific Cultural Groups Sites

CLNET, part of the Chicano/Latino Electronic Network, includes an annotated bibliography of children's literature and related resources focusing on Latinos.
http://clnet.ucr.edu/Latino_Bibliography.html

Native American Books discusses specific children's books and their accurate/inaccurate depiction of Native culture. Includes recommended lists from a Native American perspective.
http://indy4.fdl.cc.mn.us/~isk/books/bookmenu.html

Native Web, an internet community designed to foster communication, provides background information on Native American culture and extensive links to related sites.
www.nativeweb.org

REFERENCES

1. Donna E. Norton. *Through the Eyes of a Child: An Introduction to Children's Literature,* 4th ed. (Englewood Cliffs, NJ: Prentice-Hall 1995), 561.

2. Junko Yokota, "Issues in Selecting Multicultural Children's Literature," *Language Arts* (1993) 70(3): 156.

3. "Population Projections of the United States by Age, Sex, Race, and Hispanic Origin: 1995 to 2050," Washington, DC: U.S. Bureau of the Census, 1996.

4. G. Edward Evans. *Developing Library and Information Center Collections,* 3rd ed. (Littleton, CO: Libraries Unlimited 1995), 115.

5. Lyn-Miller Lachmann. *Our Family, Our Friends, Our World: An Annotated Guide to Significant Multicultural Books for Children and Teenagers.* (New Providence, NJ: Bowker 1992).

6. Lyn-Miller Lachmann. *Global Voices, Global Visions: A Core Collection of Multicultural Books.* (New Providence, NJ: Bowker 1995).

7. *Guidelines for Selecting Bias-Free Textbooks and Storybooks.* (New York: Council on Interracial Books for Children 1980), 24-5.

8. Norton, 566.

9. Beverly Slapin and Doris Seale. *Through Indian Eyes: The Native Experience in Children's Books.* (Philadelphia: New Society 1992).

10. Rudine Sims [Bishop]. *Shadow and Substance: Afro-American Experience in Contemporary Children's Fiction.* (Urbana, IL: National Council of Teachers of English 1982).

11. *Children's Catalog,* 17th ed. (New York: Wilson 1996).

12. *Middle and Junior High School Library Catalog,* 7th ed. (New York: Wilson 1995).

13. *Senior High School Library Catalog,* 14th ed. (New York: Wilson 1992).

14. *Elementary School Library Collection: A Guide to Books and Other Media,* 19th ed. (Williamsport, PA: Brodart 1995).

15. Hazel Rochman. *Against Borders: Promoting Books for a Multicultural World* (Chicago: ALA 1993).

16. Rebecca L. Thomas. *Connecting Cultures: A Guide to Multicultural Literature.* (New Providence, NJ: Bowker 1996).

17. M.V. Lindgren, ed. *The Multicolored Mirror: Cultural Substance in Literature for Children and Young Adults.* (Madison, WI: Cooperative Children's Book Center 1991).

18. Miller-Lachmann

19. Violet J. Harris. *Teaching Multicultural Literature in Grades K-8.* (Norwood, MA: Christopher-Gordon 1997).

20. Violet J. Harris. *Using Multicultural Literature in the K-8 Classroom.* (Norwood, MA: Christopher-Gordon 1992).

21. Alethea K. Helbig and Agnes Regan Perkins. *This Land is Our Land: A Guide to Multicultural Literature for Children and Young Adults.* (Westport, CT: Greenwood 1994).

22. Cooperative Children's Book Center URL: http://www.soemadison.wisc.edu/ccbc/

23. *Journal of Youth Services in Libraries* (1996) 10(1): 118.

24. Children's Book Council. *Children's Books: Awards & Prizes* (New York: CBC 1996).

25. James Rettig, "Beyond 'Cool'—Analog Models for Reviewing Digital Resources." *Online* (1996) 20(6): 52-54+. (http://www.onlineinc.com/onlinemag/SeptOL/rettig9.html); Hope N. Tillman, "Evaluating Quality on the Net" (Paper presented at Computers in Libraries Conference, Arlington, VA, 1996). (http://www.tiac.net/users/hope/findqual.html); Jan Alexander and Marsha Tate, "Teaching Critical Evaluation Skills for World Wide Web Resources," *Computers in Libraries* (1996)16(10): 49-55. (http://www.science.widener.edu/~withers/webeval.htm)

Education for Collection Development
in the Electronic Age:
With an Emphasis on Public Libraries

Vicki L. Gregory

SUMMARY. New computer-based technologies are evincing revolutionary changes in the educational curriculum for schools of library and information science, and the area of collection development is no exception. The topics discussed in the author's Collection
Development course at the University of South Florida are described, with an emphasis on the problems likely to be presented to
future public librarians as further emphasis is placed on access to
electronic forms of information. *[Article copies available for a fee from
The Haworth Document Delivery Service: 1-800-342-9678. E-mail address:
getinfo@haworthpressinc.com]*

New computer-based technologies are evincing revolutionary changes
in the educational curriculum for schools of library and information science, and the area of collection development is no exception. Although
most conceptions of the emerging electronic library of the future retain a
role for the library professional, some visionaries nevertheless question
whether the librarian's current role in respect to material selection will
continue to enjoy a place in the electronic information environment equiv-

Vicki L. Gregory is Associate Professor, School of Library and Information
Science, University of South Florida, CIS 1040, 4202 East Fowler Avenue, Tampa, FL 33620, gregory@luna.cas.usf.edu

[Haworth co-indexing entry note]: "Education for Collection Development in the Electronic Age:
With an Emphasis on Public Libraries." Gregory, Vicki L. Co-published simultaneously in *The Acquisitions Librarian* (The Haworth Press, Inc.) No. 20, 1998, pp. 185-193; and: *Public Library Collection
Development in the Information Age* (ed: Annabel K. Stephens) The Haworth Press, Inc., 1998, pp.
185-193. Single or multiple copies of this article are available for a fee from The Haworth Document
Delivery Service [1-800-342-9678, 9:00 a.m. - 5:00 p.m. (EST). E-mail address: getinfo@haworthpressinc.
com].

185

alent or analogous to the important one currently occupied in the traditional print-on-paper oriented library. Michael Malinconico in an article in
Journal of Education for Library and Information Science has contem-
plated the possibility that it may soon be the computer technologist rather
than the librarian who will control and manage electronic information
resources for future information seekers.[1] Although the key role of those
who possess the necessary mastery of a technology in controlling the ends
to which that technology is used cannot be easily discounted, the importance of such persons can also be exaggerated, as countless cautionary
tales from Mary Shelley's *Frankenstein* all the way to *Jurassic Park* have
done, but there is definitely cause for future librarians to be cognizant of
the opportunities and potential pitfalls of the electronic information environment in terms of their own career plans. Likewise, students preparing
for the electronic library cannot be allowed to overlook the continuing
importance of print. Thus, collection development coursework at the master's level must reflect a balanced approach, emphasizing technology not
as an end in itself but as a tool to use in addressing the problems collection
development tries to solve.

Ross Atkinson envisions the role of collection development in an
electronic, online environment as still consisting of the "old" roles of
discovery of resources and ranking of their comparative usefulness (resource assessment) to the patrons of the particular library in question,
with the main difference being that librarians may not in the future be
engaging in the actual acquisition of materials themselves for potential
future use, since online materials can be acquired when a user decides to
read them, but rather in providing and maintaining clear "pointers" for
the reader to use in finding what is needed. Atkinson perceives the current role of collection developers merging with and becoming a part of
the traditional roles of catalogers (bringing useful online resources to the
attention of potential users through means of bibliographic records) and
reference librarians (helping patrons find, access, and evaluate online
materials).[2]

The "Educational Policy Statement" of the Association for Library
Collections and Technical Services recognizes the problem:

> Selecting and acquiring information resources to satisfy the demand
> from library users will be more complex than is currently the case.
> These activities will require more on-the-spot decisions regarding
> the best and most efficient way to acquire information–physically or
> virtually–and will require a broad knowledge of information sources
> encompassing traditional and nontraditional publishing.[3]

However one may perceive its organization, there obviously will continue to exist a need for librarians to find and assess materials that users of a particular library serving a particular organization or geographic locale will find most useful to its needs and compatible with its purposes. The total volume of information that must be identified, sifted through and examined in order to cull the good from the not so good is increasing at such rates that library patrons will doubtless continue to need the help of information professionals in performing collection development activities, even if the concept of what the library's collection consists of changes from physical items stored on site to electronic versions of information available on computer servers throughout the world, the location of which is facilitated through the library.

To approach the teaching of collection development, I emphasize a handful of what I believe to be key topics in my course at the University of South Florida.

WHAT IS COLLECTION DEVELOPMENT?

The first topic is obviously a consideration of what it is that we are about. G. Edward Evans defines collection development as follows:

Collection development is the process of meeting the information needs of the people (a service population) in a timely and economic manner using information resources locally held as well as from other organizations.[4]

This is a broad definition that includes and recognizes the importance of the planning process and the importance of needs assessment, selection, acquisitions, planning for resource sharing, collection evaluation, weeding, and preservation, all of which I, as well as most library educators, attempt to cover in (or perhaps more accurately cram into) a three semester hour course.[5] Nevertheless, when comparing these course topics to the topics pertaining to collection development which are outlined in the ALCTS Educational Statement,[6] the ones that are purely collection development in nature are capable of being handled with reasonable thoroughness, such as knowledge of bibliographic tools and selection aids, and knowledge of the theory and skill to evaluate resources in all formats. Some of the more "peripheral," but certainly not unimportant, collection management issues, such as preservation and acquisitions, cannot be handled to the extent implied in the topic description and, therefore, might be better presented in a separate course. However, in the typical 36-hour masters program, there exists little room in the average student's course of study to allow for separate classes dealing with all the various collection management issues; thus, the one course in collection development usually must suffice, in order to allow time for the many other areas of study to which the students must be introduced.

NEEDS ASSESSMENT

Since the ultimate purpose of a library collection must be to serve the needs of its users, a statement just as true for a special collection as of a public library, the quality of the collection as perceived by its users is ultimately dependent upon the librarians' necessary understanding of who their library's users are, what their particular interests and needs are, and what these subject areas may require in terms of information and materials.

In this regard not much has really changed since 1950, when Helen Haines wrote:

> Since public library readers represent a cross section of the community, to understand community needs the librarian must have a cross-sectional knowledge of the community. . . . A surprising variety and multiplicity of contacts for the library may be developed, however, by placing upon each member of the staff the responsibility to reach some particular circle of influence. . . . The librarian's knowledge must be established by bringing together the threads that in the use of the library, are connecting people to books.[7]

To update this thought from 1950 to the present, it is only necessary to be more inclusive of electronic and other types of materials. The key matter remains "connecting" the reader to the information, no matter how the information is stored and retrieved.

Because of the importance of the needs assessment to all phases of collection development and management work, the first unit of study in my class involves a needs assessment project, which is typically done in groups of 5-7 students divided by type of library in which they are most interested. There are usually an elementary, a secondary, a public, and an academic/special library group. Students are asked to prepare a field survey and are asked to consider:

- How will you identify the respondent sample?
- What questions will be asked?

- How will you compile the information from the responses?
- How and to whom will you communicate the results of the survey?
- What actions should be taken as a result of the survey?

In the immediately following class session, the students are asked to present the results of their work orally and provide a written record of their group's efforts. Class discussion follows each group's presentation. The results of the activity should stress to students the importance of determining user needs and thereby provide them with a learning experience in how to conduct and make use of a user survey, a skill that is probably most important in public, but is applicable as well to other types of libraries.

COLLECTION DEVELOPMENT POLICIES

Because of my belief in the crucial importance of a collection development policy, the major project in the course involves the writing of and use of a collection development policy. Students are asked to prepare a collection development policy for a particular type of library, an action plan for its implementation, and, using their policy and plan, to select $2,000 worth of materials of the types covered under their collection policy.

The collection development policy that the students write is required to address the mission and objectives of the library, an analysis of subject fields, an analysis of the collection by format, as well as other important issues such as gifts, deselection and discards policies, collection evaluation/assessment, resource sharing agreements and networking, and a procedure for handling complaints and addressing censorship attempts. Last, but certainly not least, students must indicate the approval process for the policy they develop, a procedure that is too often neglected. Elizabeth Futas put the matter well:

> Today's legal environment, however, demands that library policies must be officially approved and sanctioned by the library's highest authorities in order to be recognized as in force by the courts. The trouble is that many libraries won't find out that its "unapproved" policies will not be sufficient protection against lawsuits until something terrible happens; the library will reach for its policy protection, and find out it's just a library document, not an approved policy. Then, of course, it's too late.[8]

The action plan includes such items as a statement of the main objectives sought in terms of changes to be effected as a result of the collection development policy and a procedure and timetable for implementation of the policy. The students are required to describe the strategies and techniques that will be employed in order to achieve the necessary changes implied by their policy, along with the resources, both human and material, that will be needed. Students must also devise an evaluation plan upon which the success of the policy can be measured and serve as an indicator of when the policy should be examined for needed revisions.

For the selection portion of the project, they are asked to provide an annotated bibliography of the sources they used for selection, a list of resources to be purchased with all necessary ordering information, and to indicate the source (publisher, book/serial vendor, etc.) from whom they would purchase the materials.

SELECTION:
CONTROVERSIAL LITERATURE
AND ELECTRONIC MATERIALS

For public and school librarians, in particular, selection or non-selection of controversial materials is a very important topic. In 1979, Judith Serebnick published an article reporting on a research project that found that there was a strong positive relationship between favorable book reviews and the selection of potentially controversial books by public libraries.[9] More recently Ann Curry looked at the selection or non-selection of the controversial (for its perceived high level of violence) book *American Psycho* by various Canadian Public Libraries.[10] She found that:

> Canadian librarians who did not order *American Psycho* appeared to focus on the negative comments in reviews and the media and to wait for patron demand that might compel purchase. Librarians who purchased the book appeared to focus on the presence of media attention rather than the tone of the attention. They emphasized the anticipation of demand in the selection process, rather than articulated demand, and they were willing to risk being wrong about the demand, even with a controversial book.[11]

In fact, Curry noted that the most commonly reported opinion among librarians purchasing the book was to stress the library's responsibility to provide the book so that readers could ascertain for themselves "what the media fuss was all about."[12]

The same kinds of controversies are currently raging over Internet sites.

The concern here is not so much about selection but deselection, that is, filtering the Internet. These are issues which future collection development librarians must be prepared to face; therefore, time is devoted throughout the course to intellectual freedom issues, and one class is devoted to a case study project, which is done in groups, that currently involves controversial printed materials. Questions dealing with challenges to particular titles, limited access shelving area, juvenile cards, etc., are explored in the course of working through the case study.

COLLECTION ASSESSMENT AND EVALUATION

Once librarians have selected materials for the collection, some on-going plan for collection is necessary to assess the quality of the collection, particularly for public libraries, based on the needs of the clientele of a particular library or library-system. This instructional unit includes consideration of weeding as well as taking into account needs for future selections to fill collection gaps. Students need to be introduced to both collection-centered and user-centered approaches to evaluation. Of particular importance to future public librarians are the so-called user-centered approaches, which include user surveys, circulation and in-house use studies, document delivery tests, and studies of shelf availability, and citations, as well as interlibrary loan studies.

As a result of several local collection evaluation projects, some librarians in the Tampa Bay area have become interested in cooperative collection development. In my summer 1997 class, Madison Mosley, Director of the Stetson Law Library, and my colleague, Anna H. Perrault, Associate Professor at the School of Library & Information Science at USF, visited my class to discuss with students the rationale for cooperative collection development and the approach that the Tampa Bay Library Consortium, a multitype regional network of public, academic, school, and special libraries, was considering in its initial approach in this area.

CURRENT "HOT" TOPICS

To get students acquainted with the current "burning issues" in collection development, I ask students to monitor an electronic mailing list that deals with collection development issues for several weeks, and try to encourage them to stay on such a list for the entire course, in order to use the discussions on the list as a springboard for selection of a topic for a short paper that is currently being debated by professional librarians. This past summer session, students found such issues as the outsourcing of collection development by the Hawaii State Library, Internet filtering software both pro and con, and the weeding and disposal of materials controversies such as happened in San Francisco and Philadelphia, etc. Once they had located a current topic from the mailing list, they were encouraged to go to the library literature or other appropriate sources for background and additional information. Another topic that students who were currently working in a public library setting brought into the class discussion was that of the television personality Oprah Winfrey's "Book Club" selections and the effect that media exposure generally brings to the demand for and circulation of books not previously seen to be best sellers as determined through following the traditional trade and newspaper listing services.

The variety of the topics chosen and the email and other reading that they were doing on these issues, helped to enliven discussion in many of the class sessions and make the material have more immediate pertinence to the students.

CONCLUSION

In addition to the topics outlined above, courses in Collection Development today must necessarily refer the student to issues in the acquisitions and preservation areas. But even with the restraints of time typically imposed by the Master's level classroom setting, it is possible to ensure that students get the firm grip they must have on the key issues in the field of Collection Development that will allow them to function in the key role the librarian must play in respect to directing readers to the materials they need and making sure that those materials are available, whether in print or electronic form.

REFERENCES

1. S. Michael Malinconico, "What Librarians Need to Know to Survive in an Age of Technology," *Journal of Education for Library and Information Science* 33 (Winter 1992): 226-227.

2. Ross Atkinson, "Access, Ownership, and the Future of Collection Development," in *Collection Management and Development: Issues in an Electronic Era*, edited by Peggy Johnson and Bonnie MacEwan (Chicago: American Library Association, 1994): 100-102.

3. Association for Library Collections & Technical Services, "Educational Policy Statement of the Association for Library Collections & Technical Services," Approved by the ALCTS Board of Directors, June 27, 1995, 2-3; also available in *ALCTS Newsletter* 7, no. 1 (1996): 7.

4. G. Edward Evans. *Developing Library and Information Center Collections*, 3rd. ed. (Englewood, Colo: Libraries Unlimited, 1995), 17.

5. My current syllabus is available to be viewed on the World Wide Web at: http://luna.cas.usf.edu/~gregory/lis6511.htm.

6. ALCTS, "Educational Policy Statement," 7-9; also available in *ALCTS Newsletter* 7, no. 1 (1996): 9-10.

7. Helen E. Haines. *Living with Books: The Art of Book Selection*, 2nd ed. (New York: Columbia University Press, 1950), 27-28.

8. Elizabeth Futas, ed. *Collection Development Policies and Procedures*, 3rd ed. (Phoenix: Oryx Press, 1995), 13.

9. Judith Serebnick, "An Analysis of the Relationship Between Book Reviews and the Inclusion of Potentially Controversial Books in Public Libraries," *Collection Building* 1, no. 2 (1979), 41-42.

10. Ann Curry, "*American Psycho:* A Collection Management Survey in Canadian Public Libraries," *Library & Information Science Research* 16 (Summer 1994), 201-217.

11. Ibid., 215.

12. Ibid., 215.

Staff Development for Improved Collection Management in a Rapidly Changing and Enhanced Technological Environment: Nashville Public Library's Experience

Victoria Elliott

SUMMARY. Staff development efforts at the Public Library of Nashville and Davidson County are focused on helping collection development and other staff adjust to and excel during a time of exciting technological and organizational change. Details of the staff development program are shared, with particular emphasis on topics related to collection development. *[Article copies available for a fee from The Haworth Document Delivery Service: 1-800-342-9678. E-mail address: getinfo@haworthpressinc.com]*

AS THE 21ST CENTURY APPROACHES

The staggering escalation of technological advancement over the last 30 years is an exciting dynamic in our society as a whole, and in the daily working life of the public library employee as well. However, the change that this evolution has produced can potentially create more stress and

Victoria Elliott is Staff Development Officer at the Public Library of Nashville and Davidson County, 225 Polk Avenue, Nashville, TN 37203.

[Haworth co-indexing entry note]: "Staff Development for Improved Collection Management in a Rapidly Changing and Enhanced Technological Environment: Nashville Public Library's Experience." Elliott, Victoria. Co-published simultaneously in *The Acquisitions Librarian* (The Haworth Press, Inc.) No. 20, 1998, pp. 195-202; and: *Public Library Collection Development in the Information Age* (ed: Annabel K. Stephens) The Haworth Press, Inc., 1998, pp. 195-202. Single or multiple copies of this article are available for a fee from The Haworth Document Delivery Service [1-800-342-9678, 9:00 a.m. - 5:00 p.m. (EST). E-mail address: getinfo@haworthpressinc.com].

conflict than any other type of change that a long term public library employee must tackle. Perhaps this is simply because technological innovation, more than any other change, represents the challenge of doing things differently than they have always been done before.

Public library employees have experienced change in other avenues of their working lives. Nationally, public libraries are experiencing a building "renaissance" not unlike the Carnegie years. New generations of library trailblazers are becoming our bosses and co-workers. We continue to keep the wheels of daily service turning as we look to the exciting future and development of building plans for state of the art facilities. The consequence of our growth as an institution has been that we must maintain balance between human considerations and the technology of library automation.

The traditional role of the public library has always been dictated by the ever-changing cultural differences that comprise both the needs of the customer-base and of the co-worker. Furthermore, as we have done throughout our history, the public library continues to champion and embrace the concept of being the "people's university." We make every effort to provide service to all economic groups which are reflected by a changing society and include the homeless, the mentally handicapped, young adults, the elderly, the disabled, and individuals representing all cultural or ethnic backgrounds.

LIBRARY EMPLOYEES MEET THE CHALLENGE–
AND DO IT BETTER!

Library collection management is integral to meeting customer needs within a changing society. The unprecedented growth of technology has mandated change within the daily work of the organization. Automation allows us to "do it better" by providing viable collections of print, non-print, and electronic materials for the public through improved statistical analysis, enhanced communication with the customer, and timely online acquisition of materials.

The public library's institutional goal must be to establish our role in harnessing the power of the Internet superhighway for all of society while maintaining the balance and control of any vehicles which provide information, both electronically and in print, to our public. Today's public library employee *must* be well versed in technology. So, how do we "do it better?" How do we help library employees meet the challenge of an ever-changing work environment?

LIBRARY STAFF DEVELOPMENT AT THE PUBLIC LIBRARY OF NASHVILLE AND DAVIDSON COUNTY

Phase I, Getting Started

Staff Development positions have been springing up across the country due to the importance of helping inform and educate public library employees. The coordinator of staff development can offer training that will aid both library administration and the employees responsible for collection management in obtaining a clearer understanding of the complex and varied attitudes that people have toward change.

The assistance of a staff development program in the library can support and enhance employee acceptance of the institutional transformation that occurs when technological innovations are brought to the forefront. Our human reaction to technology has aroused both enthusiasm and excitement, as well as resistance and ambivalence, among employees as they each face the change that it brings. The initial reaction of "What a fantastic invention!" is often followed by the disturbing thought "Will I be replaced?" We are then plagued further, by the equally disturbing thought of "No, you won't be replaced *if* you can keep up with this tremendous change that is now a part of your daily working existence."

Facing automation, the Public Library of Nashville and Davidson County (PLNDC) determined that our first step in training was quite basic. Everyone needed to learn how to do the work on the Innovative Interfaces (INNOPAC) automated system rather than the previously established manual one. All public service tasks changed and were enhanced by the automated system, including circulation, readers advisory, reference, acquisitions and cataloging. A group of employees consisting of both managers and line staff were selected by administration to deliver introduction to INNOPAC training to their peers. By the time all branches and departments were fully online, each public service employee had been through at least two training sessions. Acquisitions and cataloging staff had received additional training specific to their areas.

As the work itself changed with automation, employee roles began to streamline and flatten, lines of authority blurred, and our institution's balance seemed to vanish overnight. Also, like any other institution facing tremendous change, the grapevine thrived as electronic communication advanced via inter-staff email. Co-workers with technological skill bloomed and rose to the forefront of the organizational structure.

Employees began to realize the improvement and speed that INNOPAC allowed. For the first time both the public, as well as all library staff, could view and access the city library's "whole" collection of materials. The circulation of materials doubled. Inter-delivery (branch to branch by customer request) of system materials increased to the current number of 7,000 items transported per day. We found that we could now do *more*, and we could do it *faster*.

Phase II, Allocating Resources

The challenge of staff development and training in light of library automation is two-fold: assist employees in their acceptance of the institutional transformation that is occurring as we approach the 21st century; and, foster a training program that encourages the development of skills to handle the evolving work environment.

At the PLNDC our initial staff development responsibility has been to teach employees the intricacies of the tools provided by the INNOPAC system. Our library administration has made the commitment to staff development through allocated resources for peer-based training. A vacant library position has been utilized to create the position of Staff Development Officer.

The Staff Development Officer's role is to plan and coordinate training for all employees throughout the library system. Introductory training at the PLNDC has included the proper utilization of INNOPAC for daily procedures and includes circulation, library card registration, holds management, collection management, database maintenance, and the Internet. We have also tackled revitalization of the library's policies and procedures, and we continue to deliver subsequent training based on correct procedure with an emphasis on consistency of practice throughout the system.

Employees responsible for collection management have participated in classes on basic and advanced Internet techniques; deselection and weeding library collections; and, utilizing INNOPAC's "Creating Lists" function, which allows us to create a list of individual department or branch non-circulating items within specific time periods. Employees have also been encouraged to tour industry facilities, such as Ingram Book Company, and major libraries throughout the country. Collection development workshops presented by specialists in the library industry have been offered to employees with collection management responsibilities. The variety of topics that have been delivered to date have included "Intellectual Freedom and the Internet"; "Multicultural Selection"; "Centralization of Materials Selection"; and, "Review Resources: Their Strengths and Weaknesses."

Phase III, Gathering More Tools

As we have begun to master the intricacies of our automated system, we are beginning to look for ways to improve the system itself by tuning it to meet our own needs. Our acquisitions staff has refined the online ordering process and our Collection Development Administrator and her staff are exploring ways to adapt various technologies to meet our own process needs.

We also have begun to investigate selection tools available to us in the world at large, via the Internet. Sample sites that we have found to be useful include: "Amazon, Earth's Biggest Bookstore" claims 2.5 million titles and offers both formal and subjective reviews (http://www.amazon.com); "Educate Online" has the award-winning "CD-Rom Review Pages" and also offers book reviews (http://www.educate.co.uk); and, "Shoestring Radio Theatre" is an excellent site for movie reviews (http:www.shoestring.org). From these home pages the selector can get to many other linked sites of interest for collection development.

An important step in assimilating changing technologies and their impact on collection management has been the establishment of committees to explore all aspects of the system. Collection development issues are examined and resolved through a committee comprised of representative library administrators, managers, and line-staff responsible for either juvenile or adult materials selection. The group is currently rewriting the library's selection policy. The committee continues to review and enhance selection procedures as we look to the future and it also alerts library administration to staff development and training needs in collection management.

Phase IV, Planning for the Future

Training the selector for success is currently an important staff development goal at the PLNDC. Our materials selection team includes both the seasoned employee as well as those who are new to collection management. It is important to provide continuing education for long term selectors. They, in turn, will take a lead role in training new selectors. Training should emphasize the organizational culture of the library, tools for enhanced subject knowledge, methods of keeping abreast of the publishing world, the shifting paradigms of electronic and print media, and communication and time management skills.

Basic level training must focus on policies and procedures, guidelines for selection and deselection in the public library, print and electronic review sources, budgeting guidelines, and participation in a mentor program with a seasoned selector.

Advanced training should be offered on subjects such as institutional planning and goal setting; the roles that collection evaluation, assessment, and the INNOPAC system each play in creating viable collections; and vanguard technological resources. Also, all teams of selectors will continue to explore improved and centralized procedures for the selection process.

IN CONCLUSION, COMING FULL CIRCLE

The Nashville Public Library is currently embarking on an ambitious building project including a new main library and five new regional branches. The INNOPAC system has allowed us to see the efficiencies that are now available to us. We have become comfortable with the universal statistical truths that the computer reveals to us. Centralization of selection of library materials is not a taboo subject for our employees at this point because they realize that they are not being "replaced" by technology.

The psychology of change has moved full circle at the PLNDC. Experience has taken us from the initial automation process including employee training on change and automated procedure, to our current status within an organization planning its own very bright future.

SIDEBAR MATERIAL-1

Public Library of Nashville and Davidson County at a Glance

Statistics

Branches and Special Services	23
Staff	209.7 FTE
Population Served	527,200
Holdings Per Capita	1.3
Funding Per Capita	$19.59
Materials $ Per Capita	$2.72
Annual Budget (FY96/97)	$10.3 Million
New Funding for Capital Improvements	$98 Million Approx

Staff Development and Training Highlights

Staff Development 1996:	28 Courses In-House
Technology, Collection Development,	
Managerial and New Employee Tracks	

Collection Development Track	56 Professionals and Para-Professionals

Training Delivered 1996:

Managing Change	16 Hours
Internet-Intro	2 Hours
Internet-Advanced Search Engines	2 Hours
Deselection	4 Hours
Collection Development and Selection	12 Hours

SIDEBAR MATERIAL-2

Automation Highlights

- The prolonged advancement in library automation and technological development at PLNDC began with the installation of an integrated online system, INNOPAC, in March 1994.

- The Innovative Interfaces (INNOPAC) automated system provides an online public catalog, acquisitions with electronic ordering and materials booking, serials control, circulation, and a gateway to the Internet with staff Internet email.

- The library's holdings are in full MARC format and are indexed in the online system database. OCLC, which has been in use since 1979, is the source of MARC records.

- Public access to online services is provided in house and by 24-hour dial-in service which includes: a public catalog with patron-placed holds, patron self-renewal by self-viewing of the circulation record, access to magazine indexing, and full text via the EBSCO Masterfile and Full Text 1000.

- Access to an Internet gateway including a locally mounted text browser of the World Wide Web and library-sponsored Web pages has been available since February 1995. A Web interface for the public catalog came online on April 15, 1996; and, two workstations providing graphic access to the Web at the Main Library became available shortly following its debut.

- In 1997, 5 CD-ROM workstations were established within a homework center library located in a public housing area; online service on the Bookmobile through a cellular link was introduced; and, a community information database made its debut.

- In Fall 1997, multi-library networking began with the Athena Project: a cooperative effort by Nashville area university, public, and school libraries. Using SiteSearch software concurrent catalog searches can occur at all venues employing Z39.50 technology.

- Immediate automation plans call for the installation of additional graphic access workstations in larger branch libraries. Long-range plans include providing graphic access to the Internet at branch libraries and providing local history indexes online with images.

FURTHER READING

About PLNDC

"Nashville Revival," by Donna D. Mancini. *Library Journal*, May 15, 1997, p. 38-39.

"Peeling the Onion: Nashville Public Library's Team Approach to Developing and Maintaining a Website," by Pam Reese. *Tennessee Librarian*, Volume 48, Number 4, Winter 1996/97, p. 18-25.

Statistical Report 1997: Public Library Data Service. Chicago: Public Library Association, 1997.

"Tennessee Library and Information Technologies: Metropolitan Public Libraries," by Rita Hamilton. *Library HiTech*, Issue 54-55-14: 2 (1996), p. 279-286.

About Collection Development Training and the Human Aspect of Library Automation

Guide for Training Collection Development Librarians. Susan L. Fales, Editor. Collection Management and Development Guides, No. 8. Chicago: American Library Association, 1996.

Human Aspects of Library Automation. Hilary Dyer with Anne Morris. Gower Publishing Company, 1990.

Index

T - #0539 - 101024 - C0 - 229/152/12 - PB - 9780789013361 - Gloss Lamination